Learn-the-Alphabet
Arts & Crafts

**Easy Letter-by-Letter Arts and Crafts Projects
That Turn Into Beautiful Take-Home ABC Books**

by Roberta Willenken

with Piper Lawrence and Beverly Cione

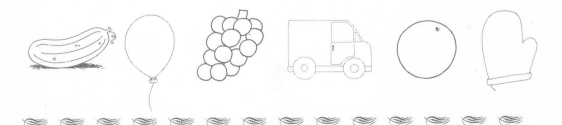

SCHOLASTIC
PROFESSIONAL BOOKS

Dedication

To all of the Blue Room children, who worked hard and had fun all the way from A to Z, especially Mathieu, whose enthusiasm helped this book happen.

Acknowledgments

My family, Lou, Chris, and Tim could not have been more supportive—I couldn't have pursued my dreams without them.

No teacher could possibly hope to work in a more collaborative, creative, and stimulating environment, and I thank everyone at the 92nd Street Y Nursery School for their encouragement and support. Special thanks to Nancy Schulman, Ellen Birnbaum, Marcia Thaler, Lynne Rosen, Erica Friedman Katz, Lisa Powell, Brenda Ratliffe, and Terri Resnick, all of whom provided lively conversation and ideas for this book.

ISBN # 0-439-16354-4
Copyright © 2000 by Roberta Willenken
All rights reserved.
Printed in the U.S.A.

Cover design by
Norma Ortiz

Interior design by
Holly Grundon

Interior illustrations by
Rusty Fletcher

Interior photographs by
Roberta Willenken,
Piper Lawrence, and
Beverly Cione

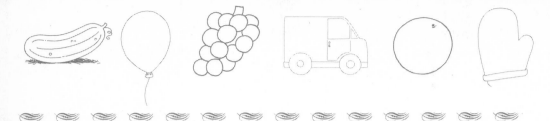

Contents

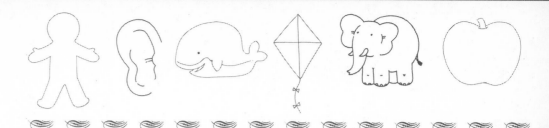

Contents

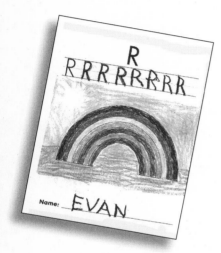

Name: EVAN

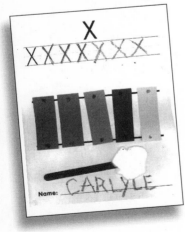

Name: CARLYLE

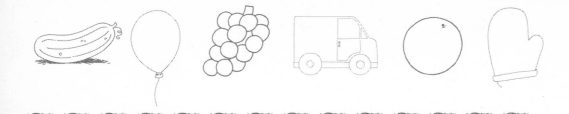

Introduction

In our busy and energetic pre-kindergarten classroom, introducing the alphabet is an important part of our curriculum. To make a yearlong alphabet study exciting for children, we decided to have each child "publish" his or her very own appealing alphabet book, using arts and crafts as well as skill-enhancing activities. The resulting children's ABC books promote letter recognition and awareness of sound-symbol correspondence.

The impact these books have on learning in our classroom is extraordinary! The children adore watching their books "grow" throughout the year. We display the ABC books in a prominent place, so children can check them out each morning. The books also serve as a wonderful focal point for classroom visitors, giving them a chance to see and appreciate the work the children do. In addition, each book is an invaluable tool for evaluating a child's progress and for sharing with parents during conferences.

Sending our books home near the end of the year is a major event for the children. They are proud to have their work compiled in such a special way. The positive feedback we get from parents underscores the importance of this project.

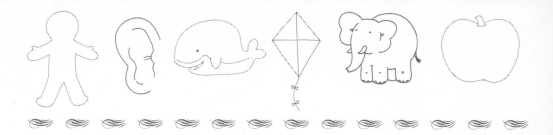

Teaching With This Book

The activities in this book can easily be incorporated into almost any existing alphabet curriculum. You don't have to do all of the activities, but you'll find them enjoyable and easy enough to add to your classroom routines.

We encourage you to develop your own routine for presenting each letter of the alphabet. Our approach works well for us—it is designed to reach each child's skill level, whether the children are just beginning to learn letter names, associate sounds and letters, or are beginning to read.

Keep in mind that young children learn at different rates and in different ways. Presenting the alphabet should always include visual, auditory, and tactile components. For example, we show children what each letter looks like, we sound out the letter and give examples of words that begin with that letter, and we provide arts-and-crafts activities that reinforce the letter.

Starting the Project

Before you let the children know that they will be making alphabet books, you may want to try out a few letters first. Just have the children complete the activities, then display and save their work. This way, you can assess students' skill level and see how the process works in your class before making a yearlong commitment. That's how we began!

After completing the first three or four letters, we invited the children to create a watercolor painting for a "special project." We then assembled the work they've done so far into books, put their names and paintings on the covers, and gathered together for a special time. We showed the group

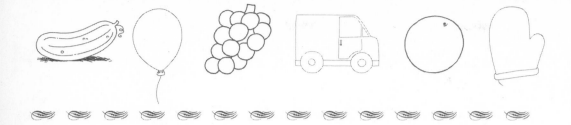

several alphabet books that we found in our school. After we discussed the characteristics of an alphabet book, we gave the children our big surprise: Each of them was already making his or her own alphabet book to take home at the end of the year! The children were very excited to see their work already in their books, and they never lost their enthusiasm throughout the year. To celebrate this special occasion, we had alphabet cookies and juice.

Making the Books

There are many different ways of making the children's books. To make ours, we put together 29 9-by-12-inch pages for each child and bound them in a spiral binder at the beginning of the year. (We use precut railroad board in a variety of colors from JL Hammett. It is inexpensive and holds up unbelievably well through a year of handling.)

Here's another alternative:

1. For each child, put together 29 sheets of 9-by-12-inch construction paper (two for the front and back covers, one for an index or table of contents, and 26 for the letters of the alphabet).
2. Punch holes in the pages and use loose-leaf rings, ribbon, yarn, or pipe cleaners to hold the pages together.
3. Write a child's name on each book cover.
4. Invite each child to make a drawing or watercolor painting. Glue the drawing or painting to the child's book cover.

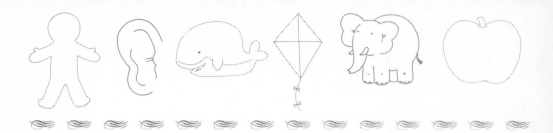

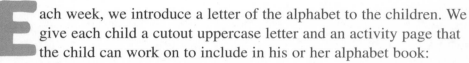

Filling the Alphabet Books

Each week, we introduce a letter of the alphabet to the children. We give each child a cutout uppercase letter and an activity page that the child can work on to include in his or her alphabet book:

- Children decorate the letter using arts and crafts that reinforce the letter. For example, they make apple prints on A's, or glue ribbons on R's.
- On the activity page, children trace and print the assigned letter. They also complete an arts-and-crafts activity that helps reinforce the letter sound. For example, gluing paper gum balls in a gumball machine for the letter G, or assembling a dinosaur for D.

To make cutout letters for children, photocopy the letter patterns at the back of this book on card stock or tag board. Then, cut out the letter and use it as a pattern for cutting out more letters from construction paper.

When the children finish decorating their letters, we glue the cutout letters to 8 1/2-by-11 paper. You can display them on the wall or bulletin board if you wish. At the end of the week, we take each child's decorated letter and activity sheet and glue them on two facing pages in the child's book. (Leave the first two pages blank for the title page and table of contents.)

At the end of the year, we add the title page at the front of the book that shows our school name, the school year, and a list of the letter-related activities (see page 13).

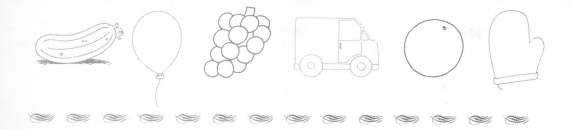

Introducing the Letters in Your Classroom

When presenting each letter to the class, we use one child's book to recall our progress so far—it's a great way to review the letters and their associated sounds.

We have a 3-by-3-foot bulletin board, which we use to display the letter of the week and pictures of things that begin with that letter. We cut the upper- and lowercase letters that we display from 12-by-18-inch paper.

During group meeting, we introduce the letter of the week by removing the upper- and lowercase letters from the board and showing them to the children. We hold up the uppercase letter and ask, "Does anyone know the name of this letter?" Children adore thinking of new names for the letters—capital A becomes "big A," "mommy A," "daddy A," and even "uppercase A."

Next, we ask if anyone knows the sound that capital A makes. We have the children repeat the sound in a group, often injecting humor into the repetition. Then, we ask the same questions for lowercase a (also known in our classroom as "small a," "tiny a," and "baby a"). We then have children think of words that begin with the letter A. The pictures on the board are a great starting point.

We have included ideas for presenting each letter. But the most important thing is to find a routine that works for your group. Remember that young children learn new things best when they are presented in a fun and engaging way.

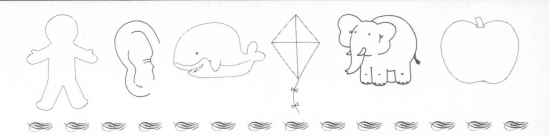

Activities for the Week

In addition to making the books, we have a variety of activities that help reinforce each letter of the alphabet:

⑥ ABC Movement Game

We have made a set of 4-by-6-inch cards with large uppercase letters printed on them. We have at least six copies of each letter. We arrange a few cards to feature the letter we are learning about. Then, we have the children stand in the middle of the room and tell them, "When you see an A, run in place, when you see a B, tap your head, when you see a C, clap your hands, and when you see an X, sit down." We always end the game with X so the children are seated and ready for the next activity.

⑥ Letter Bag

We have a small, white laundry bag decorated with letters. We fill it with 5 to 10 objects that begin with the letter of the week and are easily recognizable. We always include a picture of any child or teacher whose name begins with the letter. We use the objects in the bag to encourage discussion and sharing of information. We ask, for example, "Who knows something about an apple? an ambulance? an airplane?" At the end, we make a list of the things we had found in the bag. (In a kindergarten classroom, this list activity might be expanded in many ways, including displaying the list on the alphabet board, or incorporating it into a homemade "Big Book" for the class.)

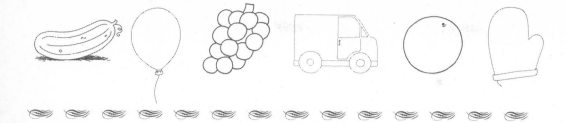

⑥ Art Activities

We use supporting art activities when they present themselves. A high-light for B is Bear Day, when each child brings a bear friend to school, and we do bear collages and a dot-to-dot bear during activity time.

⑥ Read a Book

Find books that feature characters or main ideas that are related to the letter of the week. See page 12 for a list of suggested books—one for each letter of the alphabet.

Some More Thoughts

⑥ Never miss an opportunity to explore sound with the children. Careful listening activities, whether or not they are alphabet-related, help promote phonemic awareness and are an important part of mastering sound-symbol correspondence.

⑥ Always be as encouraging as possible when teaching letter sounds to children. It is important to be aware, and try to convey to the children, that the rules sometimes don't work. This is especially important with letters like C, K, S, and all of the vowel sounds. Telling a child that he or she is wrong—kitten does not start with a C—after you've presented the sound is confusing. We always say something like, "That's great listening. Kitten does begin with the sound we're learning about, even though it starts with a different letter."

⑥ Make it personal and fun. Include the children at all levels and they will have a good foundation for learning.

⑥ Our most important advice for teaching young children is to be sure to combine ritual with plenty of room for spontaneity. Learning should be lots of fun! The emphasis should be on having each child learn new things. Avoid having rigid goals for what they need to learn.

Letter-Perfect Books From A to Z

Here's a partial list of books you can share with students as they master each letter of the alphabet:

A **Imogene's Antlers**
by David Small (Crown, 1985)

B **Drawing Lessons From a Bear**
by David McPhail (Little Brown, 2000)

C **The Very Hungry Caterpillar**
by Eric Carle (Putnam, 1984)

D **How Do Dinosaurs Say Goodnight?**
by Jane Yolen (Scholastic, 2000)

E **Edward the Emu**
by Sheena Knowles (HarperTrophy, 1998)

F **Fish Is Fish**
by Leo Lionni (Knopf, 1987)

G **The Grouchy Ladybug**
by Eric Carle (HarperCollins, 1996)

H **A House for Hermit Crab**
by Eric Carle (Simon & Schuster, 1988)

I **Isaac the Ice-Cream Truck**
by Scott Santoro (Henry Holt, 1999)

J **Jamberry**
by Bruce Degen (Harperfestival, 1995)

K **Koko's Kitten**
by Francine Patterson (Scholastic, 1987)

L **Lyle, Lyle Crocodile**
by Bernard Waber (Houghton Mifflin, 1987)

M **The Mitten**
by Jan Brett (Putnam, 1989)

N **Noisy Nora**
by Rosemary Wells (Puffin, 2000)

O **The Big Orange Splot**
by Daniel Pinkwater (Scholastic, 1993)

P **Pete's a Pizza**
by William Steig (HarperCollins, 1998)

Q **The Keeping Quilt**
by Patricia Polacco (Simon & Schuster, 1998)

R **The Rainbow Fish**
by Marcus Pfister (North South Books, 1995)

S **Stone Soup**
by Ann McGovern (Scholastic, 1987)

T **Tikki Tikki Tembo**
by Arlene Mosel (Henry Holt, 1989)

U **Ugh**
by Arthur Yorinks (Sunburst, 1993)

V **The Velveteen Rabbit**
by Margery Williams Bianco (Henry Holt, 1999)

W **Amos & Boris**
by William Steig (Sunburst, 1992)

X **A Xylophone for X-Ray Fish**
by Liza Charlesworth (Scholastic, 2000)

Y **Yertle the Turtle and Other Stories**
by Dr. Seuss (Random House, 1988)

Z **On Beyond Zebra**
by Dr. Seuss (Random House, 1980)

ALPHABET BOOKS:

ALPHA-TALES: A Series of 26 Irresistible Animal Storybooks That Build Phonemic Awareness & Teach Each Letter of the Alphabet by various authors (Scholastic, 2000)

Alpha Bugs by David A. Carter (Little Simon, 1994)

The Ocean Alphabet Book by Jerry Pallotta (Charlesbridge, 1990)

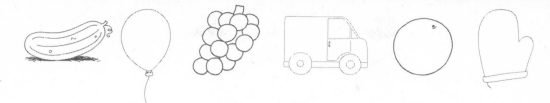

My Alphabet Book

A	. . . . .	Apple prints	. . . . .	Apple collage
B	. . . . .	Balloon prints	. . .	Balloons
C	. . . . .	Corn prints	. . . .	Cookies
D	. . . . .	Dots	. . . .	Dinosaur
E	. . . . .	Egg paints	. . . . .	Envelope with E pictures
F	. . . . .	Fingerpaints	. . . .	Fruit bowl with fruits
G	. . . . .	Glitter paint	. . . .	Gum balls
H	. . . . .	Hearts	. . . . . .	House of shapes
I	. . . . .	Ice paint	. . . . .	Ice-cream cone
J	. . . . .	Jell-O sprinkles	. .	Jack-in-the-box
K	. . . . .	Key rubbings	. . . .	Kites
L	. . . . .	Lipstick	. . . . . .	Lion
M	. . . . .	Marble painting	. .	Mittens
N	. . . . .	Newspaper	. . . .	Necklace
O	. . . . .	O's	. . . .	Octopus
P	. . . . .	Prints	. . . . . .	Pizza
Q	. . . . .	Q-tip painting	. .	Quilt
R	. . . . .	Ribbon	. . . . . .	Rainbow
S	. . . . .	String paints	. . .	Snowman design
T	. . . . .	Toothpicks	. . . .	Tic-tac-toe
U	. . . . .	Umbrella collage	. .	Underwear
V	. . . . .	Vines	. . . .	Van
W	. . . . .	Wood	. . . .	Whale
X	. . . . .	X-rays	. . . . . .	Xylophone
Y	. . . . .	Yarn	. . . .	Yellow collage
Z	. . . . .	Zebra stripes	. . .	Zipper bag with Z pictures

Introducing the Letter A

Present a capital and lowercase A at group time. Hold up the capital letter and ask, "Who knows the name of this letter?" *(A)*

Introduce the idea that the letter A makes different sounds when it is in a word. One sound is the same as the name of the letter. Ask, "Can anyone guess what that sound is?" Give examples of words that start with the long-a sound, such as apron, acorn, April, Amy. Next, ask if anyone knows another sound that the letter A makes. Give examples of words that begin with the short-a sound, such as apple, alligator, ambulance, etc.

Repeat the activity with lowercase a.

Making Apple-Print A's

You'll need:
- **A** pattern (page 68)
- apples
- plastic knives
- red, green, and yellow paint
- small paper or plastic plates

1 Use the A pattern to cut out the letter from white construction paper for each child. (Optional: Tape the cutout letter to a sheet of waxed paper to make it easy for children to paint and handle.) Write the child's name on the back of each letter before handing it out.

2 Tell children that they will use apples to paint their A's. Pour a small amount of red, green, and yellow paint on paper or plastic plates. Use a separate plate for each color.

3 Using plastic knives, help children cut the apples into thick slices. Then show them how to dip an apple slice in the paint and make a print on the paper. Use a different slice for each color. (Some children may try to "paint" with the apple by moving it across the paper. Have the children dab the apple slices on the paper to cover their A's with apple prints.)

4 When the paint dries, glue the apple-print A's to 8 1/2-by-11 paper. You may want to display the A's on the wall or bulletin board before gluing them in the children's books.

Want to make it simpler?
Cut small apple shapes from red, yellow, and green construction paper and have children glue them on their A's.

Using the Activity Page

Name MEGAN

You'll need:

- **A** activity page (page 69)
- small pieces of red, yellow, and green construction paper
- glue sticks
- markers

1 Photocopy the activity page on white paper for each child.

2 Show children how to print A's on the printing line by tracing the light-gray A's with a marker. Encourage them to try printing on their own at the end of the line. Have children write their names at the bottom of the page, or offer to do it for them.

3 Have children glue the colored pieces of paper to the apple on their activity pages to make a collage.

Want to make it simpler?

Distribute red-, yellow-, and green-colored collage stickers for students to decorate their apples.

Things for the "A" Bag

Fill a bag with the following objects. Take out one object at a time, and invite children to identify it and share something they know about the object.

- apple
- apron
- ant
- alligator
- airplane
- acorn
- ambulance
- photo of anyone in your class whose name begins with A
- any other object that begins with A

Movement Game

Assemble 4-by-6-inch letter cards in the following order:

Ask children to stand and follow these instructions:

- When you see an A, run in place.
- When you see any other letter, tap your head.
- When you see an X, sit down.

Try These Other A-Related Activities:

- Anything with apples—taste them and graph favorite kinds, cook with them, count them, and so on.
- Sing *The Ants Go Marching*.

- Pretend to be ants crawling on the ground to music.
- Bring an airplane to group time, and invite children to talk about flying on an airplane.

Bb

Introducing the Letter B

Present a capital and lowercase B at group time. Hold up the capital letter and ask children, "Who knows the name of this letter?" *(B)*

Next, ask if anyone knows what sound the letter B makes. Give examples of words, such as ball, balloon, and bubbles. Find fun ways to reinforce the B sound. For example, blow pretend b-b-b-b-b-b-bubbles. Or, you might want to hand out balloons and have children bounce them to the sound of the letter. Invite children to give examples of words that begin with the letter B.

Repeat the activity with lowercase b.

Making Balloon-Printed B's

You'll need:

- **B** pattern (page 70)
- small, softly inflated balloon for each child
- assorted paints in squeeze bottles (red, blue, green, yellow, purple, etc.)
- small paper plates

1 Use the B pattern to cut out the letter from white construction paper for each child. (Optional: Tape the cutout letter to a sheet of waxed paper to make it easy for children to paint and handle.) Write the child's name on the back of each letter before handing it out.

2 Children will have a great time covering their B's with balloon prints. Help children select two or three paint colors and squeeze a small amount—about the size of a quarter—near the center of a plate. The colors should be next to each other.

3 Show children how to use the balloon in a bouncing motion. Tell the children to "bounce" the balloon on the plate and then onto their B's. Repeat this process until most or all of the letter is covered. Remind children to use the balloon in an up-and-down motion, instead of side to side. They will be delighted with the unique way the colors mix together on their letters.

4 When the paint dries, glue the balloon-printed B's to 8 1/2-by-11 paper. You may want to display the B's on the wall or bulletin board before gluing them in the children's books.

Want to make it simpler?

Have the children paint the B's in different shades of blue. Mix the paints with the group.

Using the Activity Page

1 Photocopy the activity page on white or light-blue paper for each child. Use the balloon pattern to cut out five balloons from different-color paper for each child.

2 Show children how to print B's on the printing line by tracing the light-gray B's with a marker. Encourage them to try printing on their own at the end of the line. Have children write their names at the bottom of the page, or offer to do it for them.

3 Show children how to glue a balloon to the end of each string. When they are done, have children count the balloons with you to make sure they each have five.

You'll need:
- ⊚ **B** activity page (page 71)
- ⊚ balloon pattern (page 120)
- ⊚ glue sticks
- ⊚ markers

Want to make it simpler?
Draw the balloons on the activity page before photocopying it. Then have children color in the balloons.

Things for the "B" Bag
Fill a bag with the following objects. Take out one object at a time, and invite children to identify it and share something they know about the object.

- ⊚ bears
- ⊚ banana
- ⊚ bubbles
- ⊚ balls
- ⊚ bread
- ⊚ buttons
- ⊚ balloon
- ⊚ book
- ⊚ beans
- ⊚ block
- ⊚ photo of anyone in your class whose name begins with B
- ⊚ any other object that begins with B

Movement Game
Assemble 4-by-6-inch letter cards in the following order:

Ask children to stand and follow these instructions:
- ⊚ When you see a B, run in place.
- ⊚ When you see an A, tap your head.
- ⊚ When you see an X, sit down.

Try These Other B-Related Activities:

- ⊚ Sing *B-I-N-G-O*.
- ⊚ Have children act out *Teddy bear, Teddy bear, Turn around* . . .
- ⊚ Play with balls.
- ⊚ Blow bubbles.
- ⊚ Use straws to "blow" paint on paper.
- ⊚ Bake banana bread.
- ⊚ Have a Bear Day! Invite children to bring their bear friends to school. Then create bear collages.

Introducing the Letter C

Present a capital and lowercase C at group time. Hold up the capital letter and ask children, "Who knows the name of this letter?" *(C)*

Explain to children that, like the letter A, C makes different sounds. For now, however, they're going to learn only one of those sounds. Give examples of words, such as cat, cookie, carrot, and camera. Ask, "Can anyone guess the sound the letter C makes?" (You can also ask if anyone knows what other letter makes the same sound, but children may get confused.)

Find fun ways to reinforce the letter sound. Eat a pretend cookie and have the children make the sound c-c-c-c-c each time you take a bite. Let the children take turns being the leader at this. Then, invite them to give more examples of C words.

Repeat the activity with lowercase c.

Making Corny C's

1 Use the C pattern to cut out the letter from white construction paper for each child. (Optional: Tape the cutout letter to a sheet of waxed paper to make it easy for children to paint and handle.) Write the child's name on the back of each letter before handing it out.

2 Tell children that they will use corn to paint their C's. Pour different-color paints on each plate. Show the children how to roll corn in the paint and then onto their letter. Use a different piece of corn for each color. They will enjoy seeing the pattern the kernels make. Remind them to roll the corn rather than paint with it.

3 When the paint dries, glue the corn-painted C's to 8 1/2-by-11 paper. You may want to display the C's on the wall or bulletin board before gluing them in the children's books.

You'll need:
- ⊚ **C** pattern (page 72)
- ⊚ several ears of raw corn
- ⊚ 3 different colors of paint
- ⊚ large plastic or paper plates

Want to make it simpler?
Cut out colorful collage pieces and have children create a collage on their C's.

Using the Activity Page

Name BENJAMIN

You'll need:
- **C** activity page (page 73)
- 6 white 1-inch circles (cut from construction paper or use stickers)
- 6-by-3-inch metallic paper or aluminum foil
- markers
- glue sticks

1 Photocopy the activity page on white paper for each child.

2 Show children how to print C's on the printing line by tracing the light-gray letters with a marker. Encourage them to try printing on their own at the end of the line. Have children write their names at the bottom of the page, or offer to do it for them.

3 To make a "cookie tray," have children glue the metallic paper or aluminum foil at the center of their sheets. Then, have them glue their white circle "cookies" on the tray and decorate them with markers.

Want to make it simpler?
Draw a cake or a cupcake on the sheet before copying and have the children color and decorate it.

Things for the "C" Bag
Fill a bag with the following objects. Take out one object at a time, and invite children to identify it and share something they know about the object.

- corn
- can
- coffee
- crayon
- crown
- comb
- carrot
- cake or cupcake
- car
- candle
- camera
- photo of anyone in your class whose name begins with C
- any other object that begins with C

Movement Game
Assemble 4-by-6-inch letter cards in the following order:

Ask children to stand and follow these instructions:
- When you see a C, clap your hands.
- When you see an A, run in place.
- When you see a B, tap your head.
- When you see an X, sit down.

Try These Other C-Related Activities:

- Have carrots for snack.
- Play *Who Took the Cookie From the Cookie Jar?*
- Make collages.
- Use clothespins to sort small objects.
- Talk about cars and where we like to go in them.

Introducing the Letter D

Present a capital and lowercase D at group time. Hold up the capital letter and ask, "Who knows the name of this letter?" *(D)*

Next, ask if anyone can guess what sound the letter D makes. Give examples of words, such as dog, doll, and drum. Find fun ways to reinforce the D sound. For example, tap out a simple rhythm on a drum while making the d-d-d-d-d sound. Invite children to repeat the rhythm when you're done. Ask them to give examples of words that begin with the letter D.

Repeat the activity with the lowercase d.

Making Dotted D's

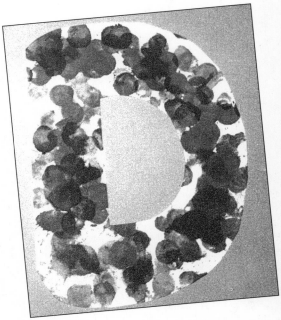

1 Use the D pattern to cut out the letter from white construction paper for each child. (Optional: Tape the cutout letter to a sheet of waxed paper to make it easy for children to paint and handle.) Write the child's name on the back of each letter before handing it out.

You'll need:
- **D** pattern (page 74)
- dot paint markers or bingo markers

2 Tell children that they will be covering their D's with dots. Using dot paint markers or bingo markers is the easiest and most fun way to do this. You can also use cotton balls dipped in small cups of paint. Try to use bright colors that will mix well. Remind children to cover most of their letter with colored dots.

3 When the paint dries, glue the dotted D's to 8 1/2-by-11 paper. You may want to display the D's on the wall or bulletin board before gluing them in the children's books.

Want to make it simpler?
Use plastic droppers to color the D's with drops of food coloring or liquid watercolors.

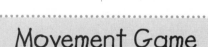

Using the Activity Page

You'll need:
- ☺ **D** activity page (page 75)
- ☺ dinosaur pattern (page 120)
- ☺ glue sticks
- ☺ brass fasteners
- ☺ markers or stickers

1 Photocopy the activity page on white paper for each child. Use the pattern to cut out a dinosaur from yellow or blue paper for each child. Punch a hole in the dinosaur head and body pieces where indicated.

2 Show children how to print D's on the printing line by tracing the light-gray letters with a marker. Encourage them to try printing on their own at the end of the line. Have children write their names at the bottom of the page, or offer to do it for them.

3 Show children how to use a brass fastener to assemble their dinosaur. Encourage children to decorate their dinosaurs with markers or stickers. Then, have children glue the dinosaur's body to the sheet. Be sure to tell children not to glue the head and neck, so the dinosaur's head can move up and down.

Things for the "D" Bag

Fill a bag with the following objects. Take out one object at a time, and invite children to identify it and share something they know about the object.

- ☺ dinosaur
- ☺ dog
- ☺ dice
- ☺ drum
- ☺ dish
- ☺ doll
- ☺ diaper
- ☺ doughnut
- ☺ daisy
- ☺ dump truck
- ☺ photo of anyone in your class whose name begins with D
- ☺ any other object that begins with D

Movement Game

Assemble 4-by-6-inch letter cards in the following order:

Ask children to stand and follow these instructions:
- ☺ When you see a D, run in place.
- ☺ When you see a B, tap your head.
- ☺ When you see a C, clap your hands.
- ☺ When you see an X, sit down.

Try These Other D-Related Activities:

- ☺ Have doughnuts at snack time.
- ☺ Tap rhythms on drums.
- ☺ Sing *Five Little Ducks.*
- ☺ Play *"What's Behind the Door?"*: Make a door that opens and closes from tag board. Use Velcro to fasten familiar objects behind the door. Give children clues and ask them to guess what's behind the door. The child who guesses correctly opens the door and takes the object.

Ee

Introducing the Letter E

Present a capital and lowercase E at group time. Hold up the capital letter and ask, "Who knows the name of this letter?" *(E)*

Explain to children that E is one of those letters that sometimes has the same sound as its name. Give examples of words that start with the long-e sound, such as eagle, easy, easel, and evening. Ask children, "Does anyone know another sound that the letter E makes?" Give examples of short-e sounds, such as egg and elephant.

Find fun ways to reinforce the E sound. For example, have an envelope filled with E's. Encourage children to make the long-e or short-e sound every time you take out an E. Or, invite the children to move like elephants, swinging their "trunks" to music.

Repeat the activity with the lowercase e.

Making Eggy E's

You'll need:
- **E** pattern (page 76)
- a dozen egg yolks
- different-color food coloring or liquid water-color
- plastic cups
- plastic spoons
- big paint-brushes

1 Use the E pattern to cut out the letter from white construction paper for each child. (Optional: Tape the cutout letter to a sheet of waxed paper to make it easy for children to paint and handle.) Write the child's name on the back of each letter before handing it out.

2 Show children the eggs and tell them that they will make paint from egg yolks. Egg paint is fun to use—it's thick and dries with a beautiful sheen and smooth finish. Put two egg yolks in a cup and add a few drops of red food coloring or liquid water color.

Repeat with other colors. Let the children help mix the egg paints.

3 Have the children paint their E's with egg paint. Remind them to cover the entire letter.

4 When the paint dries, glue the egg-painted E's to 8 1/2-by-11 paper. You may want to display the E's on the wall or bulletin board before gluing them in the children's books.

Want to make it simpler?
Have children paint their E's at the easel using regular paints.

Using the Activity Page

Name: ADIAN

You'll need
(for each child):

- ⚙ **E** activity page
  (page 77)
- ⚙ **E** pictures
  (page 121)
- ⚙ small envelope
- ⚙ scissors
- ⚙ glue stick
- ⚙ crayons or
  markers

1 Photocopy the activity page on colored copy paper for each child. Glue a small envelope on each sheet with the flap facing out. Photocopy the E pictures on white paper for each child.

2 Show children how to print E's on the printing line by tracing the light-gray letters with a marker. Encourage them to try printing on their own at the end of the line. Have children write their names at the bottom of the page, or offer to do it for them.

3 Give each child a set of E pictures, and show how to cut on the light-gray lines to separate the pictures. Let children color the pictures before putting them in the envelope.

Want to make it simpler?
Have the children decorate the envelope and glue it on the activity sheet. Omit the additional E pictures.

Things for the "E" Bag

Fill a bag with the following objects. Take out one object at a time, and invite children to identify it and share something they know about the object.

- ⚙ envelope
- ⚙ egg
- ⚙ ear
- ⚙ earring
- ⚙ elephant
- ⚙ elastic
- ⚙ eraser
- ⚙ photo of anyone in your class whose name begins with E
- ⚙ any other object that begins with E

Movement Game

Assemble 4-by-6-inch letter cards in the following order:

E D E C E E C D E X

Ask children to stand and follow these instructions:

- ⚙ When you see an E, run in place.
- ⚙ When you see a D, tap your head.
- ⚙ When you see a C, clap your hands.
- ⚙ When you see an X, sit down.

Try These Other E-Related Activities:

- ⚙ Taste different kinds of cooked eggs—hard-boiled, scrambled, fried. Graph favorites.
- ⚙ Have children pretend to be elephants and swing their trunks.
- ⚙ Talk about animals that hatch from eggs.
- ⚙ Take a ride in an elevator.
- ⚙ Paint at the easel.
- ⚙ Have children take turns wearing earmuffs and guessing what people are whispering to them.

Ff

Introducing the Letter F

Present a capital and lowercase F at group time. Hold up the capital letter and ask, "Who knows the name of this letter?" *(F)*

Next, ask if anyone knows what sound the letter F makes. Give examples of words, such as fan, farm, and finger. Find fun ways to reinforce the F sound. For example, show children a fan and ask them to make the sound f-f-f-f-f-f as you wave the fan back and forth. Ask children to give more examples of words that begin with the letter F.

Repeat the activity with the lowercase f.

Making Finger-Painted F's

You'll need:
- **F** pattern (page 78)
- fingerpaint paper
- different-color finger paints
- small cups

1 Use the F pattern to cut out the letter from fingerpaint paper for each child. (Optional: Tape the cutout letter to a sheet of waxed paper to make it easy for children to paint and handle.) Write the child's name on the back of each letter before handing it out.

2 Show children how they can use their fingers to paint. Hand out the paints in small cups and encourage children to use their fingers as brushes, rather than use their whole hand. Have children cover the entire letter with their finger paints.

3 When the paint dries, glue the finger-painted F's to 8 1/2-by-11 paper. You may want to display the F's on the wall or bulletin board before gluing them in the children's books.

Want to make it simpler?
Cut the F's from colored construction paper and offer children flower-shaped stickers for decoration.

Using the Activity Page

Name SOPHIE

1 Photocopy the activity page on white or colored paper for each child. Use the patterns to cut out the basket and fruit shapes from different-color paper for each child.

2 Show children how to print F's on the printing line by tracing the light-gray letters with a marker. Encourage them to try printing on their own at the end of the line. Have children write their names at the bottom of the page, or offer to do it for them.

3 Have the children glue their basket and colored fruits to their sheets.

You'll need:
- **F** activity page (page 79)
- fruit and bowl patterns (page 120–121)
- markers
- glue sticks

Want to make it simpler?
Draw the fruit shapes on the activity sheet before copying it. Then have the children color the fruits with markers.

Things for the "F" Bag

Fill a bag with the following objects. Take out one object at a time, and invite children to identify it and share something they know about the object.

- fruit
- flowers
- fox
- foil
- fan
- fork
- fire truck
- flashlight
- fish
- frog
- flag
- feather
- photo of anyone in your class whose name begins with F
- any other object that begins with F

Movement Game

Assemble 4-by-6-inch letter cards in the following order:

Ask children to stand and follow these instructions:
- When you see an F, run in place.
- When you see an E, tap your head.
- When you see a D, walk in place.
- When you see an X, sit down.

Try These Other F-Related Activities:

- Taste different kinds of fruit. Graph favorites.
- Cover a 9-by-12-inch tag board with foil and have children paint it.
- Sing *Five Green and Speckled Frogs*.

- Talk about friends and families
- Look at feathers together. Give one to each child during group time, and experiment with the feathers. You can also use them as paintbrushes.

Introducing the Letter G

Present a capital and lowercase G at group time. Hold up the capital letter and ask, "Who knows the name of this letter?" *(G)*

Explain to children that G is another letter that makes more than one sound. For now, they are going to learn about only one of the sounds. Ask, "Can anyone guess what sound the letter G makes?" Give examples of words, such as good, glue, green, and garden.

Find a fun way to reinforce the letter sound. For example, have children answer all your questions by saying, "g-g-g-g-green." Ask, "What color is grass?" *(G-g-g-g-green)* "What color are leaves on a tree? What color do you get when you mix yellow and blue?" Our class loves silly questions, such as "What color are green beans?" or "What color is green grass?"

Repeat the activity with the lowercase g.

Making Glittery G's

1 Use the G pattern to cut out the letter from white construction paper for each child. (Optional: Tape the cutout letter to a sheet of waxed paper to make it easy for children to paint and handle.) Write the child's name on the back of each letter before handing it out.

2 Tell children that they will paint their G's with glitter paint. (If you don't have glitter paint, mix poster paint, glitter, and a small amount of glue.) Have the children cover their entire letters with glitter paint.

3 When the paint dries, glue the glittery G's to 8 1/2-by-11 paper. You may want to display the G's on the wall or bulletin board before gluing them in the children's books.

Using the Activity Page

Name: SARAH JANE

You'll need:
- **G** activity page (page 81)
- green markers
- small circles (cut from different-color construction paper or use colored circle stickers)
- glue sticks

1 Photocopy the activity page for each child on white paper.

2 Show children how to print G's on the printing line by tracing the light-gray letters with a green marker. Encourage them to try printing on their own at the end of the line. Have children write their names at the bottom of the page, or offer to do it for them.

3 Give children small circles for "gum balls." Have the children glue or stick their gum balls inside the machine on their pages. Then, invite children to color their gum-ball machines.

Things for the "G" Bag

Fill a bag with the following objects. Take out one object at a time, and invite children to identify it and share something they know about the object.

- gum balls
- goat
- ghost
- grapes
- gorilla
- guitar
- glasses
- gloves
- golf ball
- green grass
- photo of anyone in your class whose name begins with G
- any other object that begins with G

Movement Game

Assemble 4-by-6-inch letter cards in the following order:

Ask children to stand and follow these instructions:
- When you see a G, run in place.
- When you see an F, tap your head.
- When you see an E, clap your hands.
- When you see an X, sit down.

Try These Other G-Related Activities:

- Play *Duck, Duck, Goose.*
- Have children pretend to be grasshoppers and hop to music.
- Make collages with green and gold objects.
- Look at a globe.

- Ask everyone to think of something that's green.
- Taste grapes.
- Make a garden—have children decorate flowers for it.

Hh

Introducing the Letter H

P resent a capital and lowercase H at group time. Hold up the capital letter and ask, "Who knows the name of this letter?" *(H)*

Next, ask if anyone knows the sound the letter H makes. Give examples of words, such as horse, hay, and hamburger. Find fun ways to reinforce the H sound. For example, move your hand around and have children follow your hand movements while making the sound h-h-h-h-h. Ask children to give more examples of words that begin with the letter H.

Repeat the activity with the lowercase h.

Making Hearty H's

You'll need:
- ☺ **H** pattern (page 82)
- ☺ different kinds of paper (colored, patterned, wrapping paper, tissue, etc.)
- ☺ glue
- ☺ glue brush

1 Use the H pattern to cut out the letter from white or colored construction paper for each child. Write the child's name on the back of each letter before handing it out.

2 Cut small hearts from assorted papers. Have children glue the hearts to their H's. You can also suggest that they glue the hearts on top of others to create a collage effect. Help children brush a topcoat of diluted glue to help the hearts stay down on the paper.

3 Glue the heart-covered H's to 8 1/2-by-11 paper. You may want to display the H's on the wall or bulletin board before gluing them in the children's books.

Want to make it simpler?
Use heart-shaped stickers available at most educational supply stores.

Using the Activity Page

Name: WILLIAM

1 Photocopy the activity page on white or light-blue paper for each child. Use the patterns to cut out the shapes from different-color or patterned paper for each child.

2 Show children how to print H's on the printing line by tracing the light-gray letters with a marker. Encourage them to try printing on their own at the end of the line. Have children write their names at the bottom of the page, or offer to do it for them.

3 Show children how to glue the rectangles and triangle together to make a house on their sheets. Invite children to add details to their houses using markers.

You'll need:
- **H** activity page (page 83)
- house shape patterns (page 122)
- glue sticks
- markers

Things for the "H" Bag

Fill a bag with the following objects. Take out one object at a time, and invite children to identify it and share something they know about the object.

- house
- heart
- hat
- hoop
- photo of anyone in your class whose name begins with H
- any other object that begins with H
- horse
- hammer
- helicopter
- horn

Movement Game

Assemble 4-by-6-inch letter cards in the following order:

H H G H I H I G H X

Ask children to stand and follow these instructions:
- When you see an H, tap your head.
- When you see a G, run in place.
- When you see an I, walk place.
- When you see an X, sit down.

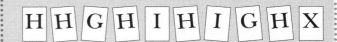

Try These Other H-Related Activities:

- Bake and decorate heart-shaped cookies.
- Have heart-shaped sandwiches at snack time.
- Play music and gallop like horses.
- Talk about houses and why we need them.
- Sing *My Hat, It Has Three Corners.*

- Make silly hats or use hats from dress-up: police hat, train hat, firefighter hat, etc. Have a child close his or her eyes, then put a hat on the child's head. Give the child clues until he or she guesses the kind of hat.

Introducing the Letter I

P resent a capital and lowercase I at group time. Hold up the capital letter and ask, "Who knows the name of this letter?" *(I)*

Explain to children that I is another letter that makes different sounds in words. One of these sounds is the same as its name. Ask, "Can anyone guess that sound?" Give examples of words that use the long-i sound, such as ice, icicle, and idea. Next, tell children that I makes another sound, as in words like igloo and insect.

Find fun ways to reinforce the I sound. Tell children about an itchy bug that goes i-i-i-i-i when it flies. Imitate a flying bug's motion with your hand and have the children repeat the I sound.

Repeat the activity with the lowercase i.

Making Icy I's

You'll need:

- ◎ **I** pattern (page 84)
- ◎ ice-cube tray
- ◎ different-color food coloring or liquid watercolor
- ◎ popsicle sticks
- ◎ aluminum foil
- ◎ warm water

1 Use the I pattern to cut out the letter from white construction paper for each child. (Optional: Tape the cutout letter to a sheet of waxed paper to make it easy for children to paint and handle.) Write the child's name on the back of each letter before handing it out.

2 A day or two before doing this activity, fill an ice-cube tray with water mixed with different colors of liquid watercolor or food coloring. Make a few cubes of each color. Cover the tray with aluminum foil and poke a popsicle stick in each cube. Then, freeze.

3 Tell children that they will paint their I's with ice cubes. Have children pick a colored ice cube with its stick and dip it in a small cup of warm water. Then have them paint their I's with the cube. Encourage children to use different colors to cover the entire letter.

4 When the paint dries, glue the ice-painted I's to 8 1/2-by-11 paper. You may want to display the I's on the wall or bulletin board before gluing them in the children's books.

Using the Activity Page

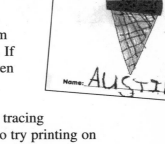

1 Photocopy the activity page on white paper for each child. Use the pattern to cut out ice-cream scoops from different-color paper. Cut out the ice-cream cone, too. If you have small red circle stickers, give them to children to use for cherries.

2 Show children how to print I's on the printing line by tracing the light-gray letters with a marker. Encourage them to try printing on their own at the end of the line. Have children write their names at the bottom of the page, or offer to do it for them.

3 Have children glue their ice-cream cones to their sheets. Have them glue one scoop of ice cream to the cone. Don't forget the cherries! Encourage children to use markers to decorate their ice cream with sprinkles.

You'll need:

- ⓖ **I** activity page (page 85)
- ⓖ ice-cream patterns (page 122)
- ⓖ small red circle stickers
- ⓖ glue sticks
- ⓖ markers

Things for the "I" Bag

Fill a bag with the following objects. Take out one object at a time, and invite children to identify it and share something they know about the object.

- ⓖ ice-cube tray
- ⓖ ice skate
- ⓖ ice-cream cone
- ⓖ iguana
- ⓖ iron
- ⓖ ink
- ⓖ insect
- ⓖ igloo
- ⓖ photo of anyone in your class whose name begins with I
- ⓖ any other object that begins with I

Movement Game

Assemble 4-by-6-inch letter cards in the following order:

I H I G I I G H I X

Ask children to stand and follow these instructions:

- ⓖ When you see an I, run in place.
- ⓖ When you see an H, tap your head.
- ⓖ When you see a G, clap your hands.
- ⓖ When you see an X, sit down.

Try These Other I-Related Activities:

- ⓖ Make and taste ice cream.
- ⓖ Talk about the process of making ice.
- ⓖ Experiment with ice: Put ice cubes on two plates, and place one indoors and the other outdoors. Ask children to predict: Will the ice melt faster indoors or outdoors?
- ⓖ Distribute rulers to children and measure objects in inches.
- ⓖ Sing *Inch by Inch*.
- ⓖ Make inkblots.

Jj

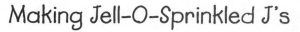

Introducing the Letter J

Present a capital and lowercase J at group time. Hold up the capital letter and ask children, "Who knows the name of this letter?" *(J)*

Next, ask if anyone can guess the sound the letter J makes. Give examples of words, such as jump, jar, jog, and Jack. Think of fun ways to reinforce the J sound. For example, if you have a jack-in-the-box, invite the children to make the sound of j-j-j-j-j-j as you turn the crank. Or, you can play a jumping game.

Repeat the activity with the lowercase j.

Making Jell-O-Sprinkled J's

You'll need:
- ⚙ **J pattern** (page 86)
- ⚙ **different colors of sugar-free Jell-O**
- ⚙ **7- or 9-oz paper or plastic cups**
- ⚙ **aluminum foil**
- ⚙ **rubber bands**
- ⚙ **diluted glue**
- ⚙ **glue brush**

1. Use the J pattern to cut out the letter from white construction paper for each child. (Optional: Tape the cutout letter to a sheet of waxed paper to make it easy for children to paint and handle.) Write the child's name on the back of each letter before handing it out.

2. Tell children that they will make "Jell-O shakers" to color their J's. To make Jell-O shakers, put some Jell-O powder in paper or plastic cups—one cup for each color. Cover the tops with foil secured with rubber bands. Punch holes in the foil to make a shaker top.

3. Show children how to completely cover their J's with diluted glue using a brush. Then demonstrate how to sprinkle Jell-O on the glue to "paint" their letters.

4. When the glue dries, glue the Jell-O-sprinkled J's to 8 1/2-by-11 paper. You may want to display the J's on the wall or bulletin board before gluing them in the children's books.

Want to make it simpler?
Help children mix the Jell-O in glue, and have them paint their letters with the mixture.

Using the Activity Page

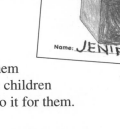

1 Photocopy the activity page on white or colored paper for each child. Photocopy and cut out the jack-in-the-box patterns for each child.

2 Show children how to print J's on the printing line by tracing the light-gray letters with a marker. Encourage them to try printing on their own at the end of the line. Have children write their names at the bottom of the page, or offer to do it for them.

3 Invite children to color the "jack" and decorate the box on the page. Show children how to fold the paper strip accordion-style to make a spring for their jack. Have them glue the jack to one end of the spring, then glue the other end to the X in the box, below the lid.

You'll need:

- J activity page (page 87)
- jack-in-the-box patterns (page 123)
- markers, crayons, or stickers
- glue sticks

Things for the "J" Bag

Fill a bag with the following objects. Take out one object at a time, and invite children to identify it and share something they know about the object.

- jacket
- jeans
- jump rope
- jelly or jam
- photo of anyone in your class whose name begins with J
- any other object that begins with J

- jaguar
- jacks
- juice box
- jelly beans in a jar

Movement Game

Assemble 4-by-6-inch letter cards in the following order:

Ask children to stand and follow these instructions:

- When you see a J, jump in place.
- When you see an H, tap your head.
- When you see an I, run in place.
- When you see an X, sit down.

Try These Other J-Related Activities:

- Put a few jelly beans in a jar and have children guess how many there are. Together, count the beans aloud.
- Taste jelly beans.
- Make Jell-O.

- Ask each child to learn a joke and share it with the class.
- Collect "junk" and make junk collages.
- Do jumping jacks, or have children pretend to be jumping beans.

Introducing the Letter K

Present a capital and lowercase K at group time. Hold up the capital letter and ask children, "Who knows the name of this letter?" *(K)*

Explain to children that K makes the same sound as another letter they've already learned about. Ask if anyone can guess the sound the letter K makes. Give examples of words, such as kite, key, and kangaroo. Ask, "What other letter makes the same sound?" *(C)*

Think of fun ways to reinforce the letter sound. For example, pretend to fly kites or use pretend keys to open locked doors. (The keys are a good introduction to the K art activity.) Ask children to give more examples of words that begin with the letter K.

Repeat the activity with the lowercase k.

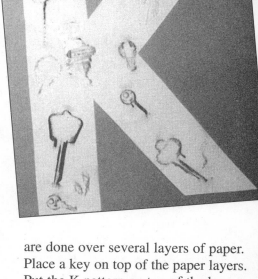

Making Key-Print K's

You'll need:
- ◎ **K** pattern (page 88)
- ◎ different-size keys
- ◎ different-color crayons
- ◎ masking tape
- ◎ extra sheets of paper

1 Use the K pattern to cut out the letter from white or yellow construction paper for each child. Write the child's name on the back of each letter before handing it out.

2 To prepare the crayons for rubbing, remove their wrappers then tape both ends with masking tape. (This makes the rubbing process so much easier for young children who tend to use the crayon as a writing tool.)

3 Show children how to make rubbings of keys. Rubbings work best if they are done over several layers of paper. Place a key on top of the paper layers. Put the K pattern on top of the key, then rub the side of a crayon over the key until the shape appears. Change keys and colors until the K is covered with key prints. Once children get the hang of this activity, they will love it!

4 Glue the key-printed K's to 8 1/2-by-11 paper. You may want to display the K's on the wall or bulletin board before gluing them in the children's books.

Using the Activity Page

1 Photocopy the activity page on white or light-blue paper for each child. Use the pattern to cut out kites from different-color paper.

2 Show children how to print K's on the printing line by tracing the light-gray letters with a marker. Encourage them to try printing on their own at the end of the line. Have children write their names at the bottom of the page, or offer to do it for them.

3 Have children glue the kites to the kite strings on their sheets. When they are finished, have them count the number of kites with you.

You'll need:
- **K** activity page (page 89)
- kite pattern (page 123)
- glue sticks
- markers

Want to make it simpler?
Draw the kites on the activity page before photocopying it. Then, have children color in the kites.

Things for the "K" Bag

Fill a bag with the following objects. Take out one object at a time, and invite children to identify it and share something they know about the object.

- kangaroo
- koala
- king
- photo of anyone in your class whose name begins with K
- any other object that begins with K

- keys on a key chain
- ketchup
- kettle

Movement Game

Assemble 4-by-6-inch letter cards in the following order:

Ask children to stand and follow these instructions:
- When you see a K, run in place.
- When you see a J, jump in place.
- When you see an H, tap your head.
- When you see an X, sit down.

Try These Other K-Related Activities:

- Talk about kangaroos.
- Do the kangaroo hop to music.
- Arrange for a kitten to visit. (Make sure no one is allergic first.)
- Make fruit kabobs.

- Pass around a crown and have children share what they would do if they were a king or queen.
- Fly kites.

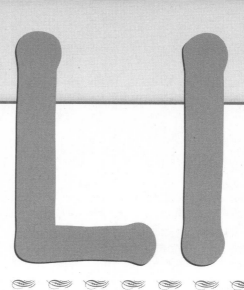

Introducing the Letter L

Present a capital and lowercase L at group time. Hold up the capital letter and ask, "Who knows the name of this letter?" *(L)*

Next, ask if anyone knows what sound the letter L makes. Give examples of words, such as letter, lollipop, and library. A fun way to reinforce the sound is by singing la-la-la-la with the group. You can have the children do it with you and then take turns at solos. Ask children to give more examples of words that begin with the letter L.

Repeat the activity with the lowercase l.

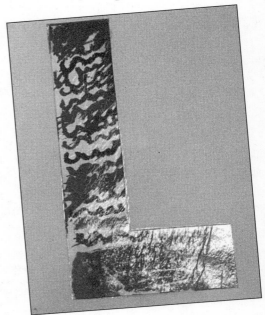

Making Lipstick-Painted L's

You'll need:
- ☺ **L** pattern (page 90)
- ☺ different-color lipsticks
- ☺ clear contact paper (optional, for each child)

1 Use the L pattern to cut out the letter from white construction paper for each child. Write the child's name on the back of each letter before handing it out.

2 Tell children that they will color their L's with lipstick. (Collect extra lipsticks from different people.) Have children "paint" their L's with different-color lipsticks. Make sure they completely cover their letters.

3 The lipstick paintings smudge very easily. Laminate the lipstick-painted L's or cover them with clear contact paper. Then, glue the L's to 8 1/2-by-11 paper. You may want to display the L's on the wall or bulletin board before gluing them in the children's books.

Want to make it simpler?
Give the children rulers and markers and have them make lines on their letter.

You'll need:

- **L** activity page (page 91)
- lion patterns (page 124)
- yellow, orange, and black construction paper
- 2-inch pieces black yarn
- markers
- 2 googly eyes or small black round stickers (for each child)
- glue sticks

Using the Activity Page

1 Photocopy the activity page on white paper for each child. Use the lion patterns to cut out pieces for each child. Cut the mane from orange construction paper, the face from yellow, and the triangle nose from black.

2 Show children how to print L's on the printing line by tracing the light-gray letters with a marker. Encourage them to try printing on their own at the end of the line. Have children write their names at the bottom of the page, or offer to do it for them.

3 Demonstrate how to glue the precut pieces and yarn to make a lion. Have them glue the googly eyes on the lion.

Want to make it simpler?
Draw the lion on the activity page before copying. Then, have children color and draw whiskers with a black marker.

Things for the "L" Bag

Fill a bag with the following objects. Take out one object at a time, and invite children to identify it and share something they know about the object.

- lion
- lemon
- ladybug
- light bulb
- ladder
- lock
- lizard
- lunchbox or lunch bag
- leaf
- lettuce
- photo of anyone in your class whose name begins with L
- any other object that begins with L

Movement Game

Assemble 4-by-6-inch letter cards in the following order:

Ask children to stand and follow these instructions:

- When you see an L, run in place.
- When you see a K, tap your head.
- When you see a J, jump in place.
- When you see an X, sit down.

Try These Other L-Related Activities:

- Sing *Mary Had a Little Lamb*.
- Have a special lunch.
- Make lemonade or lemon bread.
- Lick lollipops.
- Children enjoy learning how to print the word LOVE. Talk about things you love.
- Make a group Lego project and display.

Introducing the Letter M

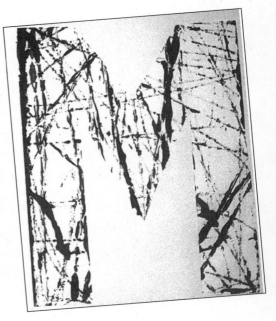

Present a capital and lowercase M at group time. Hold up the capital letter and ask, "Who knows the name of this letter?" *(M)*

Next, ask if anyone knows what sound the letter M makes. Give examples of words, such as mouse, milk, and Monday. You can reinforce the sound by acting like m-m-m-m-monkeys. Or, you can play mitten match: Cut out pairs of mittens from patterned paper. Give each child a mitten, telling him or her not to look at it until the music starts. Play some music and have the children look for someone with a mitten that matches their own. When a child finds a partner, have them sit down together. When everyone is sitting in pairs collect the mittens and play the game again.

Repeat the activity with the lowercase m.

You'll need:

- ◎ **M** pattern (page 92)
- ◎ construction paper
- ◎ plastic tray or foil baking tray
- ◎ 3 or 4 different-color paints
- ◎ small cups or bowls
- ◎ marbles
- ◎ plastic spoons

Making Marbled M's

1 Use the M pattern to cut out the letter from heavy white or colored construction paper for each child. Use removable tape to stick the letter on the construction paper. Trim the construction paper to fit in the tray. Write the child's name on the back of each letter before handing it out.

2 Tell children that they will use marbles to paint the M's. Pour a small amount of paint into cups or bowls. Drop a marble into each color. Have the children use a plastic spoon to remove the marble from the paint and put it in the tray. Show children how to tilt the tray to roll the marble over the letter. Encourage them to use different colors to paint their letters.

3 When the paint dries, glue the marbled M's to 8 1/2-by-11 paper. You may want to display the M's on the wall or bulletin board before gluing them in the children's books.

Want to make it simpler?

Buy a marbling kit to color the M's. Marbling paper is unbelievably easy and fascinating to children. They'll want to continue marbling after their M's are done!

Using the Activity Page

You'll need:

- ◎ **M** activity page (page 93)
- ◎ mitten pattern (page 124)
- ◎ small pieces of different-color paper or stickers
- ◎ glue sticks
- ◎ markers

1 Photocopy the activity page on white paper for each child. Use the pattern to cut out a pair of mittens from different-color paper for each child.

2 Show children how to print M's on the printing line by tracing the light-gray letters with a marker. Encourage them to try printing on their own at the end of the line. Have children write their names at the bottom of the page, or offer to do it for them.

3 Have the children glue the mittens on the string on their pages. They can either glue on the prepared collage paper or use stickers to decorate their mittens.

Want to make it simpler?

Draw the mittens on the activity page before copying it. Then have children color or decorate the mittens.

Things for the "M" Bag

Fill a bag with the following objects. Take out one object at a time, and invite children to identify it and share something they know about the object.

- ◎ mittens
- ◎ mouse
- ◎ map
- ◎ muffin tin
- ◎ marbles
- ◎ mask
- ◎ magazine
- ◎ magnet
- ◎ mirror
- ◎ monkey
- ◎ milk container
- ◎ photo of anyone in your class whose name begins with M
- ◎ any other object that begins with M

Movement Game

Assemble 4-by-6-inch letter cards in the following order:

Ask children to stand and follow these instructions:

- ◎ When you see an M, march in place.
- ◎ When you see an L, run in place.
- ◎ When you see a K, tap your head.
- ◎ When you see an X, sit down.

Try These Other M-Related Activities:

- ◎ March to music.
- ◎ Bake mini muffins.
- ◎ Eat macaroni and/or make macaroni collages.
- ◎ Chant *Five Little Monkeys*.
- ◎ Talk about mommies.
- ◎ Do a magic trick.

Introducing the Letter N

P resent a capital and lowercase N at group time. Hold up the capital letter and ask, "Who knows the name of this letter?" *(N)*

Ask, "Does anyone know what sound the letter N makes?" Give examples of words, such as net, nine, and necklace. Find fun ways to reinforce the N sound. For example, point to different parts of your face and have children make the n-n-n-n sound every time you point to your nose. Make noise together by making the n-n-n-n-n sound—use your arm to indicate louder or softer. Ask children to give more examples of words that begin with the letter N.

Repeat the activity with the lowercase n.

Making Newsy N's

You'll need:
- ⊚ **N** pattern (page 94)
- ⊚ newspapers
- ⊚ scissors
- ⊚ glue

1 Use the N pattern to cut out the letter from colored or black construction paper for each child. Write the child's name on the back of each letter before handing it out.

2 Tell children that they will cover their N's with pieces of newspaper. Help children cut the newspaper into small pieces. Then, have them glue the pieces on their N's.

3 Glue the news-printed N's to 8 1/2-by-11 paper. You may want to display the N's on the wall or bulletin board before gluing them in the children's books.

Using the Activity Page

Name: SETH

1 Photocopy the activity page on white paper for each child.

2 Show children how to print N's on the printing line by tracing the light-gray letters with a marker. Encourage them to try printing on their own at the end of the line. Have children write their names at the bottom of the page, or offer to do it for them.

3 Have children cut out jewel shapes from shiny paper and glue them on the necklace on their sheets. They can also decorate their necklaces with glue-on jewels.

You'll need:
- ☙ **N** activity page (page 95)
- ☙ shiny paper or small, flat glue-on jewels
- ☙ scissors
- ☙ markers
- ☙ tacky glue

Want to make it simpler?
Draw some jewels on the necklace before photocopying the activity page. Then, have the children color the jewels with glitter crayons.

Things for the "N" Bag

Fill a bag with the following objects. Take out one object at a time, and invite children to identify it and share something they know about the object.

- ☙ needle
- ☙ newspaper
- ☙ noodles
- ☙ necklace
- ☙ nightlight
- ☙ nine
- ☙ nail
- ☙ nut
- ☙ photo of anyone in your class whose name begins with N
- ☙ any other object that begins with N

Movement Game

Assemble 4-by-6-inch letter cards in the following order:

Ask children to stand and follow these instructions:
- ☙ When you see an N, run in place.
- ☙ When you see an M, walk in place.
- ☙ When you see an L, tap your head.
- ☙ When you see an X, sit down.

Try These Other N-Related Activities:

- ☙ Taste noodles.
- ☙ Talk about when we say NO.
- ☙ Bead necklaces.
- ☙ Talk about nighttime.
- ☙ Pound nails.
- ☙ Use noses (smell things).

~~~~~~~~~~~~~~~~~

Introducing the Letter O

Present a capital and lowercase O at group time. Hold up the capital letter and ask, "Who knows the name of this letter?" *(O)*

Explain that O is one of those letters that sometimes makes the same sound as its name. Give examples of words with the long-o sound, such as ocean, only, and oatmeal. Ask, "Does anyone know what other sound the letter O makes?" Show the children how their mouth makes an O shape with short-o words, such as octopus, olive, and onion. Ask children to give more examples of words that begin with the letter O.

Repeat the activity with the lowercase o.

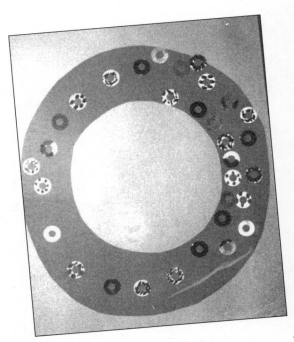

Making O-Filled O's

1 Use the O pattern to cut out the letter from orange construction paper for each child. Write the child's name on the back of each letter before handing it out.

2 Tell children that they will decorate the O's with little O's. Give each child hole reinforcements and markers. (We get the reinforcements in sheets of about 40, and give each child a whole sheet.) Have children color the hole reinforcements before sticking them to their O's.

3 Glue the O-filled O's to 8 1/2-by-11 paper. You may want to display the O's on the wall or bulletin board before gluing them in the children's books.

You'll need:
- ☺ **O** pattern (page 96)
- ☺ white hole reinforcements
- ☺ markers

Want to make it simpler?
Cut the O's from white construction paper. Give the children red and yellow paint in squeeze bottles and show them how to mix their own orange paint. Paint the O's orange.

Using the Activity Page

1 Photocopy the activity page on white paper for each child. Use the patterns to cut out the octopus head and eight legs for each child. Use different-color or patterned papers.

2 Show children how to print O's on the printing line by tracing the light-gray letters with a marker. Encourage them to try printing on their own at the end of the line. Have children write their names at the bottom of the page, or offer to do it for them.

3 Have children glue the octopus head and legs on their sheets. Together with the children, count the legs to make sure there are eight. Have children glue on the googly eyes or use small, round stickers for the eyes.

You'll need:
- **O** activity page (page 97)
- octopus patterns (page 125)
- 2 googly eyes or small, black, round stickers (for each child)
- glue sticks
- markers

Name: KATIE

Things for the "O" Bag

Fill a bag with the following objects. Take out one object at a time, and invite children to identify it and share something they know about the object.

- octopus
- orange
- onion
- owl
- oil
- olives
- oatmeal
- overalls
- photo of anyone in your class whose name begins with O
- any other object that begins with O

Movement Game

Assemble 4-by-6-inch letter cards in the following order:

Ask children to stand and follow these instructions:
- When you see an O, run in place.
- When you see an M, march in place.
- When you see an N, do nothing.
- When you see an X, sit down.

Try These Other O-Related Activities:

- Eat oranges or taste orange juice.
- Have oatmeal at snack time.
- Sing *Open Shut Them.*

- Have the children talk about what it's like to be an octopus.
- Don't forget the Oreos!

Introducing the Letter P

Present a capital and lowercase P at group time. Hold up the capital letter and ask, "Who knows the name of this letter?" *(P)*

Next, ask if anyone knows what sound the letter P makes. Give examples of words, such as popsicle, paper, and pencil. Think of fun ways to reinforce the P sound. For example, have the children pretend to be popcorn in a pot. Turn up the heat and have them p-p-p-POP! Ask children to give more examples of words that begin with the letter P.

Repeat the activity with the lowercase p.

You'll need:

- ✪ **P** pattern (page 98)
- ✪ purple and pink paints
- ✪ paintbrushes

Making Painted P's

1 Use the P pattern to cut out the letter from white construction paper for each child. (Optional: Tape the cutout letter to a sheet of waxed paper to make it easy for children to paint and handle.) Write the child's name on the back of each letter before handing it out.

2 Have children paint their P's with purple and pink paint.

3 When the paint dries, glue the painted P's to 8 1/2-by-11 paper. You may want to display the P's on the wall or bulletin board before gluing them in the children's books.

Using the Activity Page

You'll need
(for each child):
- ☺ **P** activity page (page 99)
- ☺ 6-inch circle of brown construction paper
- ☺ 5-inch circle of red construction paper
- ☺ I-inch pieces of white yarn
- ☺ glue sticks

1 Photocopy the activity page on white paper for each child.

2 Show children how to print P's on the printing line by tracing the light-gray letters with a marker. Encourage them to try printing on their own at the end of the line. Have children write their names at the bottom of the page, or offer to do it for them.

3 To make "pizza," have children glue the red circle in the middle of the brown cricle. Then, have them glue the pizza to their sheets. Show children how to glue the "cheese" yarn to their pizza.

Want to make it simpler?
Draw a pizza on the activity sheet before photocopying it. Then, have children color and decorate their pizzas.

Things for the "P" Bag
Fill a bag with the following objects. Take out one object at a time, and invite children to identify it and share something they know about the object.

- ☺ potato
- ☺ pizza
- ☺ pig
- ☺ popcorn
- ☺ pencil
- ☺ paint
- ☺ puppet
- ☺ plum
- ☺ plant
- ☺ pumpkin
- ☺ pinwheel
- ☺ photo of anyone in your class whose name begins with P
- ☺ any other object that begins with P

Movement Game
Assemble 4-by-6-inch letter cards in the following order:

Ask children to stand and follow these instructions:
- ☺ When you see a P, run in place.
- ☺ When you see an O, tap your head.
- ☺ When you see an N, do nothing.
- ☺ When you see an X, sit down.

Try These Other P-Related Activities:

- ☺ Offer a variety of P snacks—popcorn, pudding, peanuts (if no one is allergic).
- ☺ Have pizza for lunch.
- ☺ Make pudding pies.
- ☺ Make potato prints.

- ☺ Taste different kinds of cooked potatoes—baked, fries, mashed, and chips. Graph favorites.
- ☺ Have a puppet show with child-made puppets.
- ☺ Have a puppy visit.

Introducing the Letter Q

Present a capital and lowercase Q at group time. Hold up the capital letter and ask, "Who knows the name of this letter?" *(Q)*

Ask if anyone knows what sound the letter Q makes. This may be a difficult sound for children to distinguish from other letter sounds. Help them out by showing children a quilt and how it is made up of separate pieces sewn together. Explain that like the pieces of the quilt, the letter Q is usually "sewn" together to another letter, U. Give examples of words that start with these two letters, such as queen, quarter, and quilt. Ask children to think of other words that start with Q.

Repeat the activity with the lowercase q.

Making Q-Tip-Printed Q's

You'll need:
- ⚲ **Q** pattern (page 100)
- ⚲ different color paints
- ⚲ Q-tips
- ⚲ small cups or paper plates

1 Use the Q pattern to cut out the letter from white construction paper for each child. (Optional: Tape the cutout letter to a sheet of waxed paper to make it easy for children to paint and handle.) Write the child's name on the back of each letter before handing it out.

2 Tell children that they will paint their Q's using Q-tips. Put small amounts of different-color paints in cups or plates for each child. Have children use the Q-tips as paintbrushes to paint their Q's. You may want to provide an extra cup or plate for used Q-tips.

3 When the paint dries, glue the Q-tip-painted Q's to 8 1/2-by-11 paper. You may want to display the Q's on the wall or bulletin board before gluing them in the children's books.

Using the Activity Page

Name: BRITTANY

1 Photocopy the activity page on white paper for each child.

2 Show children how to print Q's on the printing line by tracing the light-gray letters with a marker. Encourage them to try printing on their own at the end of the line. Have children write their names at the bottom of the page, or offer to do it for them.

3 Have children glue the paper squares to make a quilt on their activity sheets.

Want to make it simpler?
Have the children decorate the quilt with markers.

Things for the "Q" Bag

Fill a bag with the following objects. Take out one object at a time, and invite children to identify it and share something they know about the object.

- quilt
- queen
- quarter
- question mark
- quartz
- photo of anyone in your class whose name begins with Q
- any other object that begins with Q

Movement Game

Assemble 4-by-6-inch letter cards in the following order:

Ask children to stand and follow these instructions:
- When you see a Q, run in place.
- When you see a P, tap your head.
- When you see a O, walk in place.
- When you see an X, sit down.

Try These Other Q-Related Activities:

- Talk about queens and what they do.
- Pass around a quarter. Ask children what they would buy with it.
- Play a quilt game: Have a child cover his or her eyes while another hides under the quilt. Challenge the first child to guess who is under the quilt. Repeat a few times.

- Make a class quilt: Have children decorate a felt square or make a collage on a paper square. Then, assemble all the squares into a large quilt to display.
- Play a noisy-quiet game: Have children make noise until you use a special hand signal or hold up a Q for quiet.

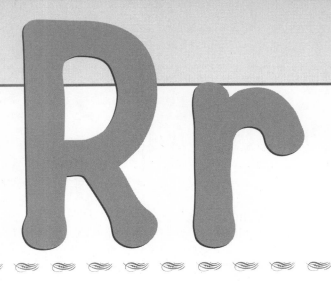

Introducing the Letter R

Present a capital and lowercase R at group time. Hold up the capital letter and ask children, "Who knows the name of this letter?" *(R)*

Next, ask if anyone knows the sound the letter R makes. Give examples of words, such as ring, ribbon, and rainbow. Find a fun way to reinforce the R sound. For example, have children r-r-r-r-roar. Or, give out ribbons and have children move with them to music. We usually present a large rainbow to help children see the colors in order, and begin to understand how they relate to one another.

Repeat the activity with the lowercase r.

Making Ribbon R's

You'll need:
- ⊚ **R** pattern (page 102)
- ⊚ different-color ribbons, about 1 to 2 inches long
- ⊚ small cups
- ⊚ glue
- ⊚ glue brushes

1 Use the R pattern to cut out the letter from red construction paper for each child. Write the child's name on the back of each letter before handing it out.

2 Tell children that they will decorate their R's with ribbons. Hand out cups of glue and glue brushes to children. Have them glue the pieces of ribbon on their R's.

3 When the glue dries, glue the ribbon R's to 8 1/2-by-11 paper. You may want to display the R's on the wall or bulletin board before gluing them in the children's books.

Want to make it simpler?
Photocopy and cut out the R pattern from white paper. Have children glue pieces of red paper on their R's.

Using the Activity Page

1 Photocopy the activity page for each child on blue paper.

2 Show children how to print R's on the printing line by tracing the light-gray letters with a marker. Encourage them to try printing on their own at the end of the line. Have children write their names at the bottom of the page, or offer to do it for them.

3 Invite children to paint the rainbow on their activity sheets. Watercolor paints work very well. In fact, most sets of 8 have the colors arranged in the order of the rainbow. (You may want to put tape over the black and brown paints to remind children not to use them.) You can also give children markers or crayons to color their rainbows. This will eliminate the need for drying time.

You'll need:
- ☺ **R** activity page (page 103)
- ☺ watercolor paints, crayons, or markers

Things for the "R" Bag

Fill a bag with the following objects. Take out one object at a time, and invite children to identify it and share something they know about the object.

- ☺ rabbit
- ☺ ring
- ☺ radio
- ☺ rice
- ☺ ruler
- ☺ ribbon
- ☺ rattle
- ☺ rope
- ☺ rock
- ☺ photo of anyone in your class whose name begins with R
- ☺ any other object that begins with R

Movement Game

Assemble 4-by-6-inch letter cards in the following order:

Ask children to stand and follow these instructions:
- ☺ When you see an R, run in place.
- ☺ When you see a P, pat your head.
- ☺ When you see a Q, be very quiet.
- ☺ When you see an X, sit down.

Try These Other R-Related Activities:

- ☺ Play music and move with ribbons.
- ☺ Make a list of things that are red.
- ☺ Paint rocks.
- ☺ Solve riddles.

- ☺ Bake rainbow cookies.
- ☺ Have raisins for snacks.
- ☺ Walk in the rain.

Introducing the Letter S

Present a capital and lowercase S at group time. Hold up the capital letter and ask children, "Who knows the name of this letter?" *(S)*

Next, ask if anyone knows the sound the letter S makes. Give examples of words, such as soup, sand, salt, and Sunday. Find a fun way to reinforce the sound. For example, have children pretend to be snakes and make the sound s-s-s-s-s-s-s. Ask children to give more examples of words that begin with the letter S.

Repeat the activity with the lowercase s.

Making Scratch-Art S's

You'll need:
- ⚙ **S** pattern (page 104)
- ⚙ scratch-art paper
- ⚙ wooden sticks

1 Use the S pattern to cut out the letter from scratch-art paper for each child. Write the child's name on the back of each letter before handing it out.

2 Have children use wooden sticks to scratch out fun designs on their S's.

3 Glue the scratch-art S's to 8 1/2-by-11 paper. You may want to display the S's on the wall or bulletin board before gluing them in the children's books.

Using the Activity Page

1 Photocopy the activity page on blue paper for each child. Use the pattern to cut out the snowman hat from black construction paper.

2 Show children how to print S's on the printing line by tracing the light-gray letters with a marker. Encourage them to try printing on their own at the end of the line. Have children write their names at the bottom of the page, or offer to do it for them.

3 Invite children to make a snowman on their activity sheets by gluing the circles and hats. Have them decorate their snowman's face with markers. (This is really fun to do in warm weather!)

You'll need:
- **S** activity page (page 105)
- snowman-hat pattern (page 125)
- 3 different-size white circles (for each child)
- black construction paper
- glue sticks
- markers

Want to make it simpler?
Draw the snowman on the activity sheet before photocopying it. Then have children color in the details.

Things for the "S" Bag
Fill a bag with the following objects. Take out one object at a time, and invite children to identify it and share something they know about the object.

- snake
- scarf
- sponge
- star
- sand
- snail
- stamp
- sock
- string
- shoe
- soap
- spoon
- photo of anyone in your class whose name begins with S
- any other object that begins with S

Movement Game
Assemble 4-by-6-inch letter cards in the following order:

Ask children to stand and follow these instructions:
- When you see an S, stamp your feet.
- When you see an R, run in place.
- When you see a Q, be very quiet.
- When you see an X, sit down.

Try These Other S-Related Activities:

- Make "stone soup."
- Pass out Styrofoam balls, and throw and catch the "snow balls" to music.
- Make sand paintings by mixing sand into paint.
- Talk about things that make us smile.
- Play STOP: Make a big stop sign. Have children walk toward you until you hold up the sign.

~~~~~~~~~~~~

Introducing the Letter T

Present a capital and lowercase T at group time. Hold up the capital letter and ask, "Who knows the name of this letter?" *(T)* Next, ask if anyone knows what sound the letter T makes. Give examples of words, such as teeth, today, and ten. Find a fun way to reinforce the sound. For example, line up the children and have them pretend to be a train that makes the sound t-t-t-t-t-t-t. You may also want to teach children how to play tic-tac-toe in preparation for the activity sheet. We bring a large tic-tac-toe board and X's and O's with Velcro on the back, and give the children a chance to learn the rules and play the game.

Repeat the activity with the lowercase t.

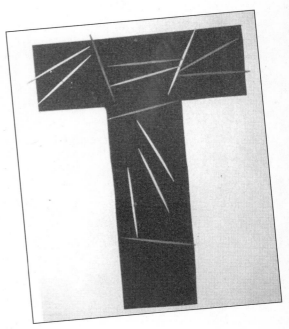

Making Toothpick T's

You'll need:
- ⓖ **T** pattern (page 106)
- ⓖ toothpicks
- ⓖ glue (tacky glue works best)

1 Use the T pattern to cut out the letter from colored construction paper for each child. Write the child's name on the back of each letter before handing it out.

2 Tell children that they will decorate their T's with toothpicks. Hand out small cups of glue. Show children how to dip both ends of the tooth- picks in glue, and then place them on the letter.

3 When the glue dries, glue the toothpick T's to 8 1/2-by-11 paper. You may want to display the T's on the wall or bulletin board before gluing them in the children's books.

Using the Activity Page

Name: LIZA

You'll need:
- **T** activity page (page 107)
- markers

1 Photocopy the activity page on white paper for each child.

2 Show children how to print T's on the printing line by tracing the light-gray letters with a marker. Encourage them to try printing on their own at the end of the line. Have children write their names at the bottom of the page, or offer to do it for them.

3 Play tic-tac-toe with each child. Show how to write X's and O's in the grid to play. Children will certainly be excited if they win!

Things for the "T" Bag

Fill a bag with the following objects. Take out one object at a time, and invite children to identify it and share something they know about the object.

- train
- truck
- tiger
- telephone
- triangle
- turtle
- toaster
- table
- toothbrush
- photo of anyone in your class whose name begins with T
- any other object that begins with T

Movement Game

Assemble 4-by-6-inch letter cards in the following order:

Ask children to stand and follow these instructions:
- When you see a T, tap your head.
- When you see an S, stamp your feet.
- When you see an R, run in place.
- When you see an X, sit down.

Try These Other T-Related Activities:

- Make triangle collages.
- Taste different foods.
- Talk about trees and paint them at the easel.
- Play telephone.
- Make a tent in which children can play.

- Take apart a broken telephone with a small group.
- Count to 10.
- Taste different kinds of tea and graph favorites.

~~~~~~~~~~~~~~~~~~~~~~~~~~~~~

Introducing the Letter U

P resent a capital and lowercase U at group time. Hold up the capital letter and ask children, "Who knows the name of this letter?" *(U)*

Tell children that U is one of those letters that make many different sounds. One sound is the same as the name of the letter—U. Give examples of long-u words, such as unicorn and useful. Next, ask if anyone knows another sound the letter U makes. Give examples of short-u words, such as umbrella, up, and under. Find a fun way to re-inforce the sound. For example, have the children grunt the sound "uh" in response to questions you ask, such as "How are you feeling?" *(Uh)* Or, have the children guess what everyone is wearing that starts with the letter U. *(Underwear)*

Repeat the activity with the lowercase u.

Making Umbrella-Covered U's

You'll need:

- ⊚ **U** pattern (page 108)
- ⊚ umbrella pattern (page 126)
- ⊚ different-color paper
- ⊚ small cups
- ⊚ glue
- ⊚ glue brush

1 Use the U pattern to cut out the letter from colored construction paper for each child. Write the child's name on the back of each letter before handing it out.

2 Tell children that they will decorate their U's with umbrella shapes. Use the pattern to cut several umbrella shapes from different-color paper. Hand out cups of glue and glue brushes to children, and have them paste the umbrellas all over their letters.

3 When the glue dries, glue the umbrella-covered U's to 8 1/2-by-11 paper. You may want to display the U's on the wall or bulletin board before gluing them in the children's books.

Using the Activity Page

1 Photocopy the activity page on white paper for each child. Use the child pattern to cut out pieces from skin-tone paper for each child. Cut out underwear from white paper as well.

2 Show children how to print U's on the printing line by tracing the light-gray letters with a marker. Encourage them to try printing on their own at the end of the line. Have children write their names at the bottom of the page, or offer to do it for them.

3 Have children select underwear for their person and glue them on. Then have them glue the person to their sheets. Encourage children to use markers to add features to their persons. Listen to them giggle as they work. (This is, without a doubt, most of the children's favorite page!)

Things for the "U" Bag

Fill a bag with the following objects. Take out one object at a time, and invite children to identify it and share something they know about the object.

- unicorn
- underwear
- umbrella
- uniform
- photo of anyone in your class whose name begins with U
- any other object that begins with U

Movement Game

Assemble 4-by-6-inch letter cards in the following order:

U U S U T U T S U X

Ask children to stand and follow these instructions:
- When you see a U, run in place.
- When you see a T, tap your head.
- When you see an S, stamp you feet.
- When you see an X, sit down.

Try These Other U-Related Activities:

- Talk about people who wear uniforms.
- Talk about things that are under the ground.
- Play an umbrella game: Bring an umbrella to group time and open it. Have the children sit in a circle and ask one child to leave the group and cover his or her eyes. Select a child to hide under the umbrella. Have the children chant, "Who is missing, who is missing? Can you tell, can you tell?" The first child returns and tries to guess who is under the umbrella.

Introducing the Letter V

Present a capital and lowercase V at group time. Hold up the capital letter and ask children, "Who knows the name of this letter?" *(V)*

Next, ask if anyone knows the sound the letter V makes. Give examples of words, such as violin, vase, and van. Find a fun way to reinforce the V sound. For example, have the children pretend to drive vans and make the sound v-v-v-v-v to represent the motor. Ask children to give more examples of words that begin with the letter V.

Repeat the activity with the lowercase v.

Making Viny V's

You'll need:
- ✿ **V** pattern (page 110)
- ✿ leaf-shape sponges, about 2 inches long
- ✿ green paint
- ✿ small plates

1 Use the V pattern to cut out the letter from white construction paper for each child. Paint a "vine stem" on the V. (Optional: Tape the cutout letter to a sheet of waxed paper to make it easy for children to paint and handle.) Write the child's name on the back of each letter before handing it out.

2 Tell children that they will paint vine leaves on their V's. Put green paint in plates for sponge printing. Show children how to dip their sponges on the paint, then lightly press them on the paper to "paint" leaves on their vines.

(Hint: Dampen sponges with a small amount of water before dipping them in paint.)

3 When the paint dries, glue the viny V's to 8 1/2-by-11 paper. You may want to display the V's on the wall or bulletin board before gluing them in the children's books.

Want to make it simpler?
Cut out green leaf shapes instead, and have the children glue them on the vine.

Using the Activity Page

1 Photocopy the activity page on white paper for each child. Use the pattern to cut out a van from different-color construction paper for each child.

2 Show children how to print V's on the printing line by tracing the light-gray letters with a marker. Encourage them to try printing on their own at the end of the line. Have children write their names at the bottom of the page, or offer to do it for them.

3 Have children glue the van on their pages. Encourage them to decorate it using markers or stickers. Then, have children draw a driver or glue their picture in the window space.

You'll need:
- ⑥ **V** activity page (page 111)
- ⑥ van pattern (page 127)
- ⑥ markers and stickers
- ⑥ glue sticks

Things for the "V" Bag

Fill a bag with the following objects. Take out one object at a time, and invite children to identify it and share something they know about the object.

- ⑥ van
- ⑥ vanilla
- ⑥ violin
- ⑥ velvet
- ⑥ Velcro
- ⑥ vest
- ⑥ vase
- ⑥ vitamins
- ⑥ visor
- ⑥ photo of anyone in your class whose name begins with V
- ⑥ any other object that begins with V

Movement Game

Assemble 4-by-6-inch letter cards in the following order:

Ask children to stand and follow these instructions:
- ⑥ When you see a V, run in place.
- ⑥ When you see a U, clap your hands.
- ⑥ When you see a T, tap your head.
- ⑥ When you see an X, sit down.

Try These Other V-Related Activities:

- ⑥ Talk about Velcro and how it works.
- ⑥ Make vanilla ice cream or vanilla pudding.
- ⑥ Vote!

- ⑥ Invite children to paint a still life of vases with flowers.

Introducing the Letter W

Present a capital and lowercase W at group time. Hold up the capital letter and ask, "Who knows the name of this letter?" *(W)*

Next, ask if anyone knows the sound the letter W makes. This is often a difficult sound for children to guess, perhaps because the sound is unrelated to the letter's name. We usually explain that the word W means two U's. Most other letters were named after the sound that the letter makes.

Find a fun way to reinforce the W sound with children. For example, tell them a story about the wind. Every time the wind blows, have the children make the w-w-w-w-w sound. Ask children to give examples of words that begin with the letter W.

Repeat the activity with the lowercase w.

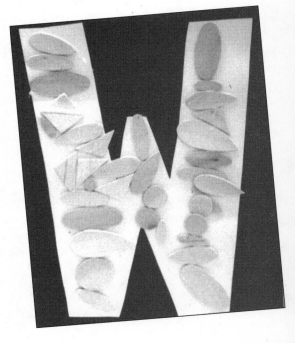

Making Woody W's

You'll need:
- ✎ **W** pattern (page 112)
- ✎ small, flat wood shapes (also known as woodles or woodsies)
- ✎ glue
- ✎ glue brush

1 Use the W pattern to cut out the letter from colored construction paper for each child. Write the child's name on the back of each letter before handing it out.

2 Show children different wooden shapes, and tell them that they will decorate their W's with the wood. Hand out cups of glue and glue brushes to children, and have them glue the wood pieces to cover their W's.

3 When the glue dries, glue the woody W's to 8 1/2-by-11 paper. You may want to display the W's on the wall or bulletin board before gluing them in the children's books.

Want to make it simpler?
Cut the W's from white construction paper or watercolor paper and have children paint them using watercolor.

Using the Activity Page

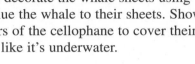

1 Photocopy the activity page on light-blue copy paper for each child. Use the pattern to cut out a whale from white paper for each child.

2 Show children how to print W's on the printing line by tracing the light-gray letters with a marker. Encourage them to try printing on their own at the end of the line. Have children write their names at the bottom of the page, or offer to do it for them.

3 Have the children color and decorate the whale sheets using markers. Then have them glue the whale to their sheets. Show them how to glue the corners of the cellophane to cover their whale. The whale will look like it's underwater.

Things for the "W" Bag

Fill a bag with the following objects. Take out one object at a time, and invite children to identify it and share something they know about the object.

- whale
- wood
- wool
- witch
- water
- wig
- watch
- wagon
- wheels
- whistle
- watermelon
- photo of anyone in your class whose name begins with W
- any other object that begins with W

Movement Game

Assemble 4-by-6-inch letter cards in the following order:

Ask children to stand and follow these instructions:
- When you see a W, walk in place.
- When you see a V, run in place.
- When you see a U, tap your head.
- When you see an X, sit down.

Try These Other W-Related Activities:

- Have watermelon for a snack.
- Make and eat waffles.
- Talk about windows and why we need them.
- Sing *Watermelon*.
- Ask the children where they would go if they had wings.
- Make white collages.
- Play with anything with wheels.

Introducing the Letter X

It's a good thing X comes near the end of the alphabet because it's a tricky one to present to young children. Bring a capital and lowercase X to group time. Hold up the capital letter and ask, "Who knows the name of this letter?" *(X)*

Explain to children that in some words, such as X-ray, X makes the same sound as its name. Find a fun way to reinforce the sound. For example, ask children to think of ways to use their fingers, arms, and legs to make the letter X. Have them make the x-x-x-x-x-x sound as they do it.

Repeat the activity with the lowercase x.

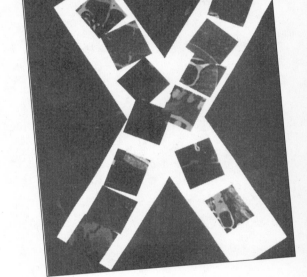

Making X-Ray X's

You'll need:
- **X** pattern (page 114)
- old X-rays (you can collect these from doctors you know)
- tacky glue

1 Use the X pattern to cut out the letter from white construction paper for each child. Write the child's name on the back of each letter before handing it out.

2 It wasn't easy coming up with an art-related activity for the letter X. Cut strips of old X-rays for children to glue on their X's.

3 Glue the X-ray X's to 8 1/2-by-11 paper. You may want to display the X's on the wall or bulletin board before gluing them in the children's books.

Want to make it simpler?
Use white crayon or oil pastel (craypas) to write X's on the X patterns before distributing them to children. Give children diluted dark-blue or black liquid watercolor in cups, and have them paint over the entire X. The white X's will magically appear!

Using the Activity Page

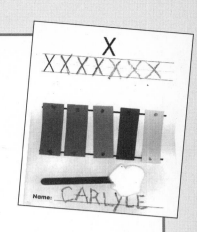

You'll need
(for each child):

- **X** activity page (page 115)
- 6 1-by-3-inch metallic craft or colored construction paper
- thin popsicle sticks
- cotton ball
- glue

1 Photocopy the activity page on white or colored paper for each child.

2 Show children how to print X's on the printing line by tracing the light-gray letters with a marker. Encourage them to try printing on their own at the end of the line. Have children write their names at the bottom of the page, or offer to do it for them.

3 To make a xylophone, have children glue the metallic craft paper "keys" on their activity pages. To make the xylophone stick, have children glue the popsicle stick and cotton ball below the xylophone.

Want to make it simpler?
Draw in the xylophone keys on the activity sheet before copying, then have children color in the keys.

Things for the "X" Bag

The X bag is a real stretch. You may want to put in things that have an X in the middle of the word. Take out one object at a time, and invite children to identify it and share something they know about the object.

- xylophone
- X-ray
- exit sign
- taxi
- fox
- photo of anyone in your class whose name begins with X
- any other object that begins with X

Movement Game

Our kids couldn't wait for this one because all through the year, X meant sit down. Assemble letter cards in the following order:

Ask children to stand and follow these instructions:

- When you see an X, sit down.
- When you see an R, run in place.
- When you see a T, tap your head.
- When you see a W, walk in place.

Try These Other X-Related Activities:

- Pass around a xylophone, and have children tap out rhythms.
- Play "X marks the spot": Put a large X somewhere in the classroom. Have the children ask you questions until someone guesses the location of the X. Have that child get the X and hide it in another location. Then play all over again.

Introducing the Letter Y

Present a capital and lowercase Y at group time. Hold up the capital letter and ask children, "Who knows the name of this letter?" *(Y)*

Explain to children that Y makes a sound that is very different from its name. Tell them you don't know "Y"! (They may get the joke.) Ask if anyone knows what sound the letter Y makes. Give examples of words, such as yo-yo, yellow, and yak. Find a fun way to reinforce the sound. For example, show them a yo-yo and have them make the y-y-y-y-y-y-y sound as you use the yo-yo. Ask them to give more examples of words that begin with the letter Y.

Repeat the activity with the lowercase y.

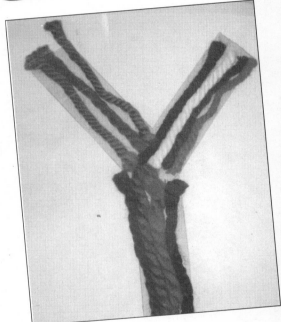

Making Yarn-Covered Y's

You'll need:
- ◎ **Y** pattern (page 116)
- ◎ 4-inch pieces of different-color yarn
- ◎ glue

1 Use the Y pattern to cut out the letter from white or yellow construction paper for each child. Write the child's name on the back of each letter before handing it out.

2 Tell children that they will cover their Y's with yarn. Have children glue the yarn to their Y's. Ask them to cover the entire letter and to use the yarn in straight pieces.

3 Glue the yarn-covered Y's to 8 1/2-by-11 paper. You may want to display the Y's on the wall or bulletin board before gluing them in the children's books.

You'll need:
- **Y** activity page (page 117)
- different kinds of yellow paper (construction, patterned, textured, or wrapping paper)
- 6-inch square black construction paper (for each child)
- glue sticks
- markers

Using the Activity Page

1 Photocopy the activity page on white paper for each child.

2 Cut out the yellow paper in different shapes and sizes to make a yellow collage.

3 Show children how to print Y's on the printing line by tracing the light-gray letters with a marker. Encourage them to try printing on their own at the end of the line. Have children write their names at the bottom of the page, or offer to do it for them.

4 Have the children glue the black square at the middle of their pages. Then, have them glue the cut yellow paper on the square to make a collage.

Things for the "Y" Bag

Fill a bag with the following objects. Take out one object at a time, and invite children to identify it and share something they know about the object.

- yarn
- yogurt
- yam
- yield sign
- photo of anyone in your class whose name begins with Y
- any other object that begins with Y
- yo-yo
- yam
- yardstick
- yak
- yeast

Movement Game

Assemble 4-by-6-inch letter cards in the following order:

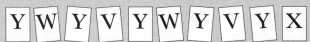

Ask children to stand and follow these instructions:
- When you see a Y, run in place.
- When you see a W, walk in place.
- When you see a V, tap your head.
- When you see an X, sit down.

Try These Other Y-Related Activities:

- Talk about things you make with yarn.
- Make a list of things that are yellow.
- Taste yogurt or yams.
- Teach the children to yodel.
- Show them the word "YES," and ask the class yes-or-no questions.

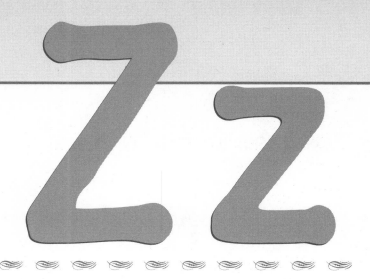

Introducing the Letter Z

Present a capital and lowercase Z at group time. Hold up the capital letter and ask, "Who knows the name of this letter?" *(Z)*

Next, ask if anyone can guess the sound the letter Z makes. Give examples of words, such as zipper, zero, and zoo. Find a fun way to reinforce the Z sound. For example, tell children to put on "pretend" jackets and zip them up and down, making the z-z-z-z-z sound.

Repeat the activity with the lowercase z.

Making Zebra-Stripe Z's

You'll need:
- ◎ **Z** pattern (page 118)
- ◎ black rolling paint markers or black paint

1 Use the Z pattern to cut out the letter from white construction paper for each child. (Optional: Tape the cutout letter to a sheet of waxed paper to make it easy for children to paint and handle.) Write the child's name on the back of each letter before handing it out.

2 Tell children that they will paint zebra stripes on their Z's. Show them how to use rolling paint markers with

black paint in them. Or, they can paint stripes using a thin brush with black paint.

3 When the paint dries, glue the zebra-stripe Z's to 8 1/2-by-11 paper. You may want to display the Z's on the wall or bulletin board before gluing them in the children's books.

Using the Activity Page

Name: STEPHANIE

You'll need:
- ⊚ **Z** activity page (page 119)
- ⊚ Z pictures (page 127)
- ⊚ small plastic zipper bag (for each child)
- ⊚ scissors
- ⊚ crayons or markers

1 Photocopy the activity page on white or colored copy paper for each child. Photocopy the Z pictures on white paper for each child.

2 Glue the plastic zipper bag to each activity page. (You can even find some that make a zipper sound!)

3 Show children how to print Z's on the printing line by tracing the light-gray letters with a marker. Encourage them to try printing on their own at the end of the line. Have children write their names at the bottom of the page, or offer to do it for them.

4 Have children cut apart the Z pictures along the dotted lines and color them. Then, have them put the pictures in the zipper bag.

Things for the "Z" Bag

Fill a bag with the following objects. Take out one object at a time, and invite children to identify it and share something they know about the object.

- ⊚ zebra
- ⊚ zero
- ⊚ zucchini
- ⊚ zipper bag
- ⊚ zig-zag
- ⊚ zipper
- ⊚ zoo sign or picture
- ⊚ photo of anyone in your class whose name begins with Z
- ⊚ any other object that begins with Z

Movement Game

Assemble 4-by-6-inch letter cards in the following order:

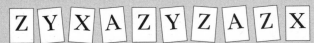

Ask children to stand and follow these instructions:
- ⊚ When you see a Z, run in place.
- ⊚ When you see a Y, touch your toes.
- ⊚ When you see an A, do something silly.
- ⊚ When you see an X, sit down.

Try These Other Z-Related Activities:

- ⊚ Invite each child to act out an animal at the zoo, and have the other children guess the animal.
- ⊚ Talk about how zippers work.
- ⊚ Play math games using zero.

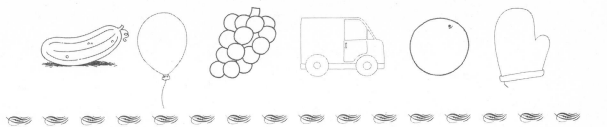

Letter
Patterns
&
Activity
Pages

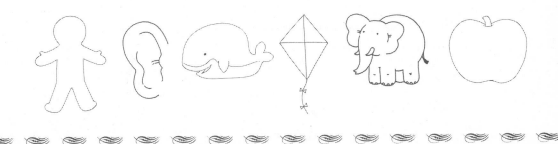

68

A

A A A A A A

Name: _____

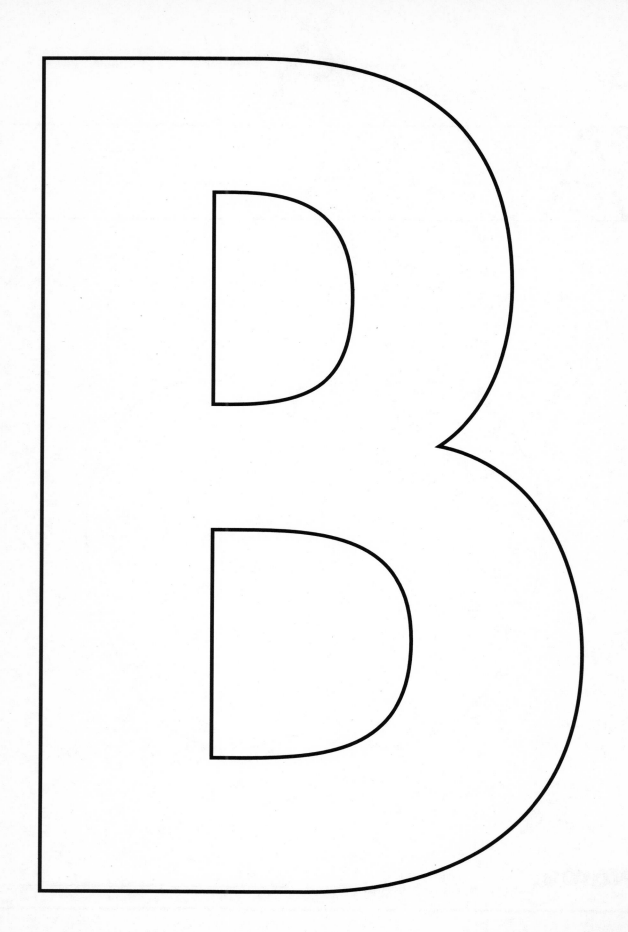

B

B B B B B

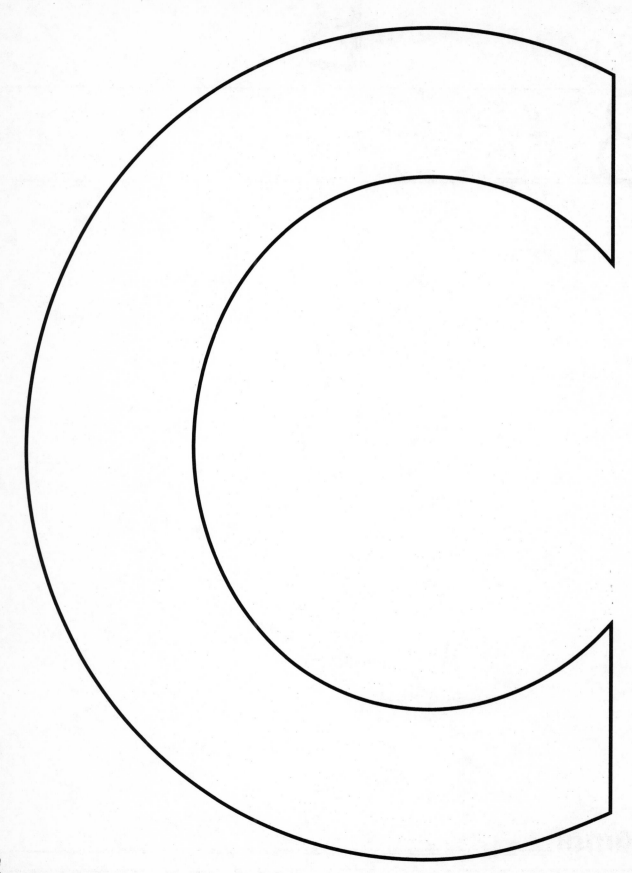

72

C

C C C C C

Name:_____

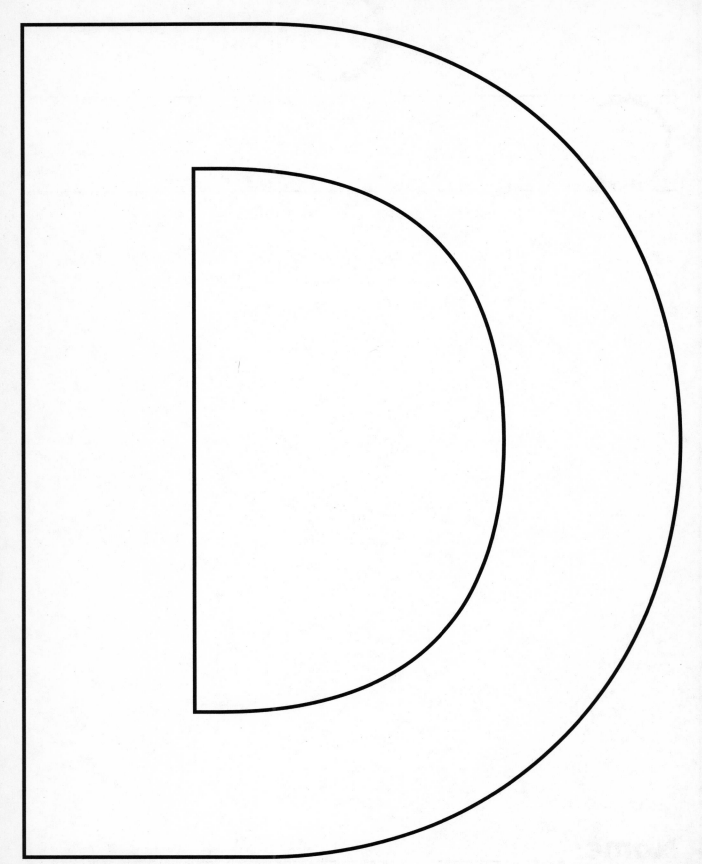

74

D

D D D D D

Name:_____

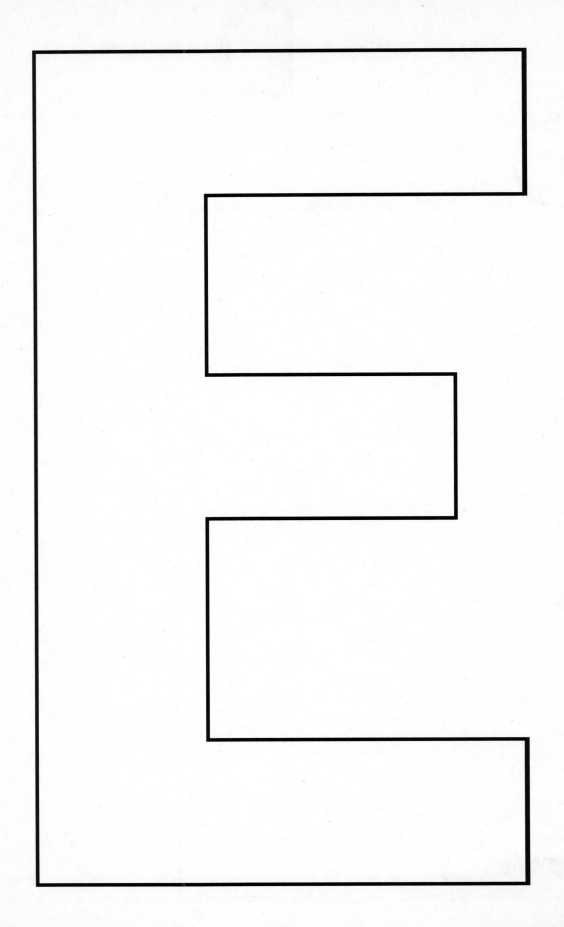

E

E E E E E

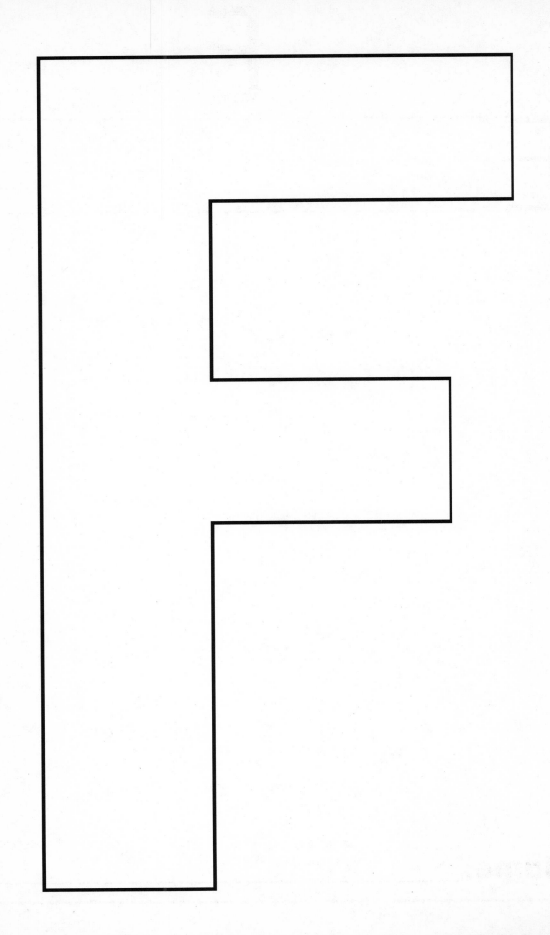

F

F F F F F

Name:_____

80

G

G G G G G

Name:_____

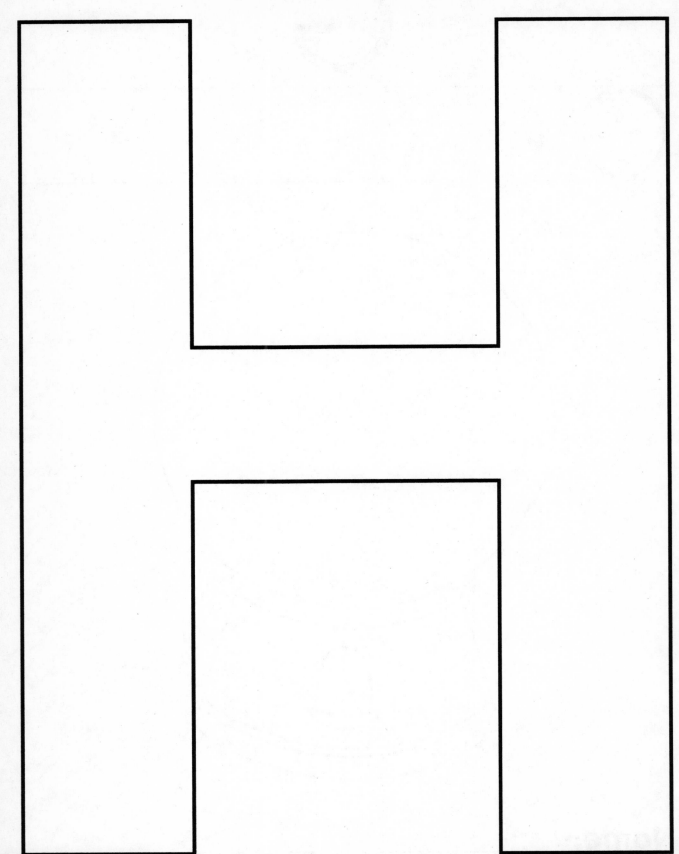

82

H

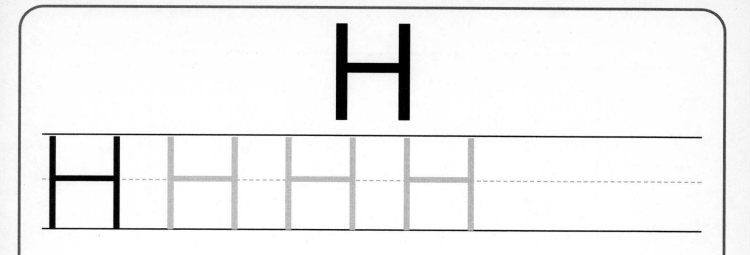

Name:_____

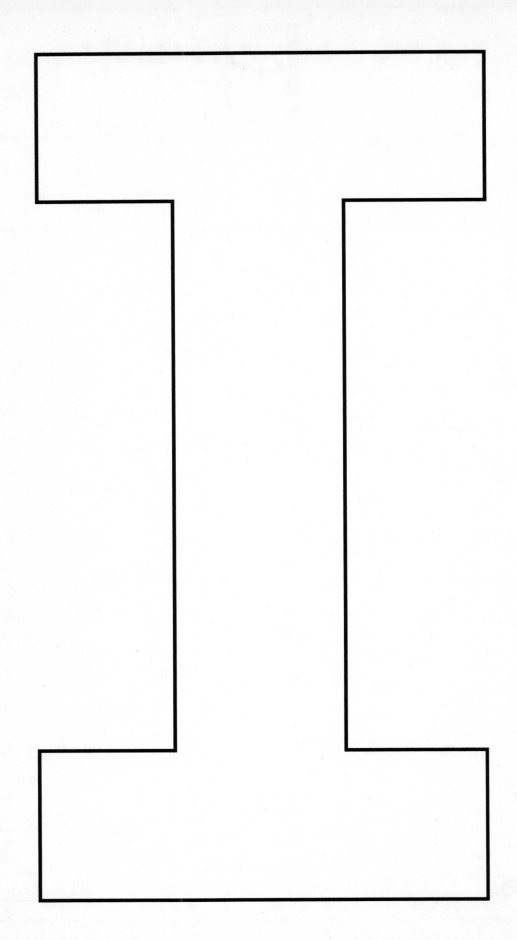

84

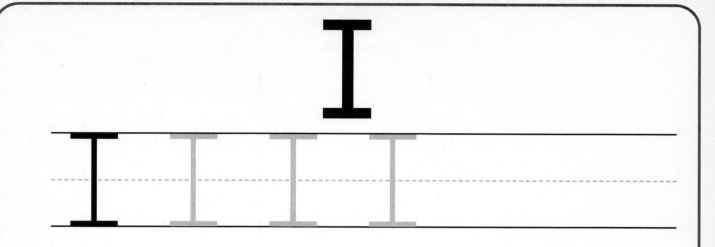

Name:_____

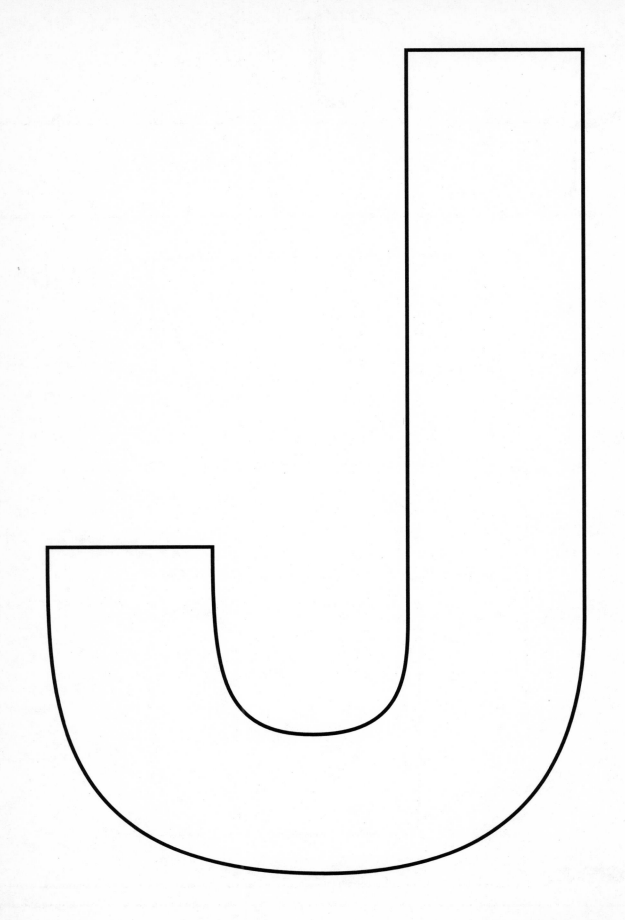

J

J J J J J

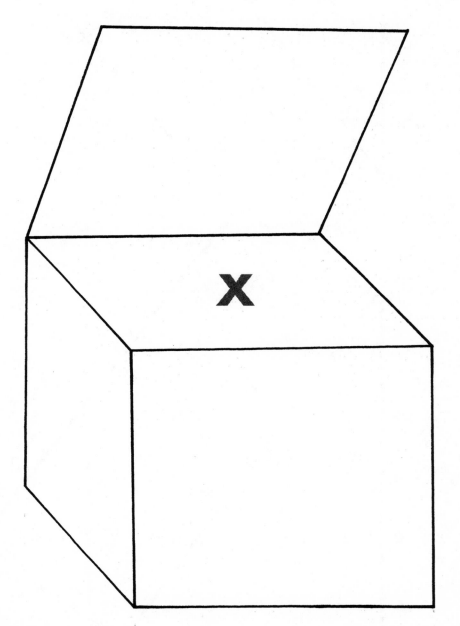

x

Name:_____

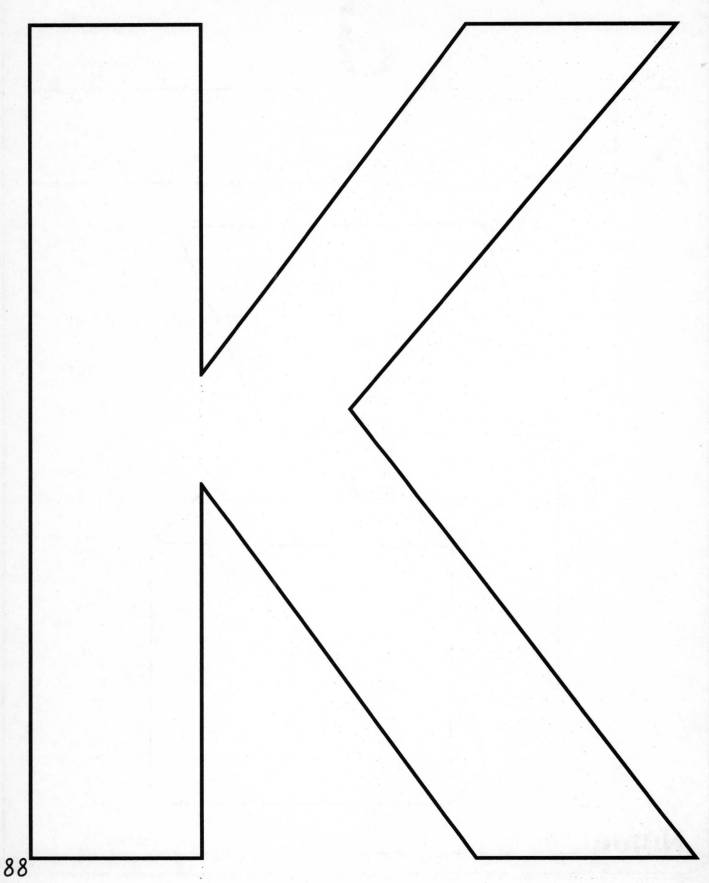

K

K K K K

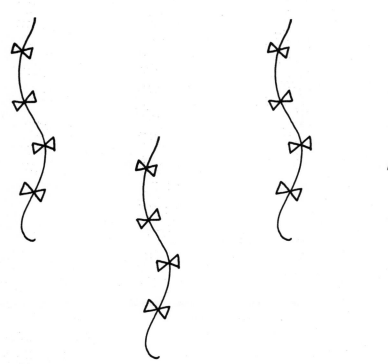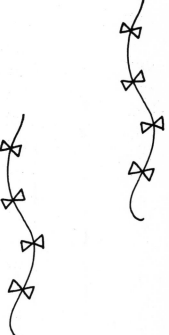

Name:_____

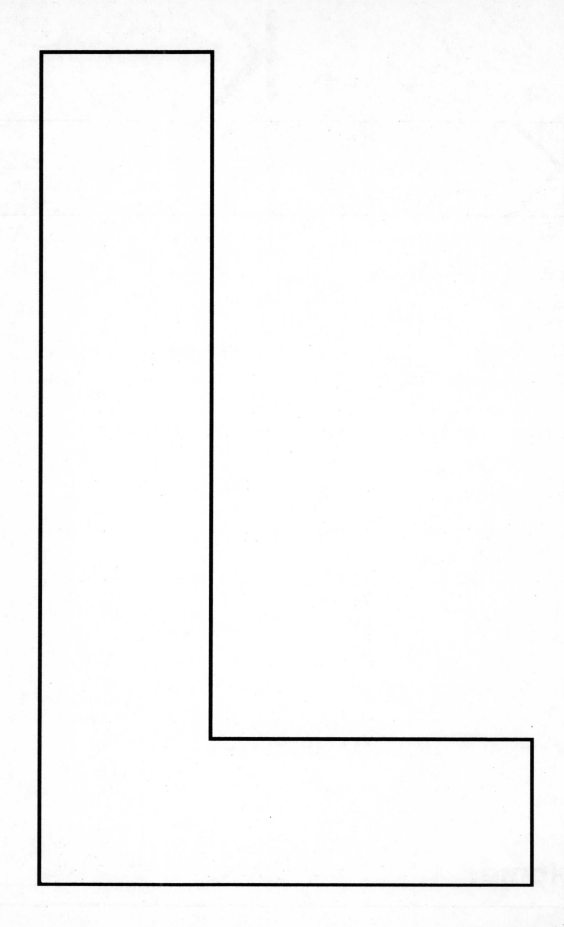

L

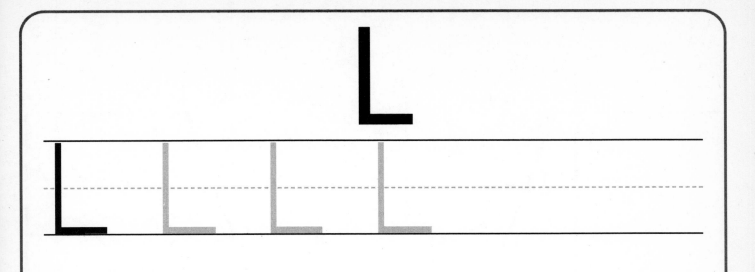

92

M

M M M M M

Name:_____

94

N

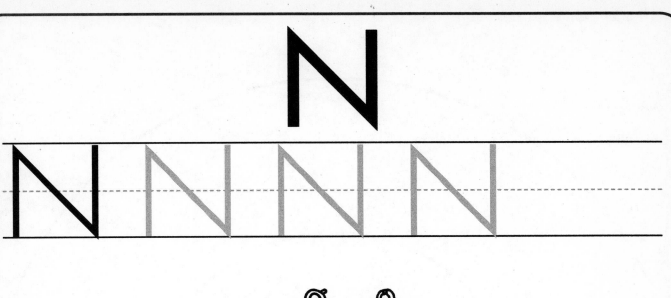

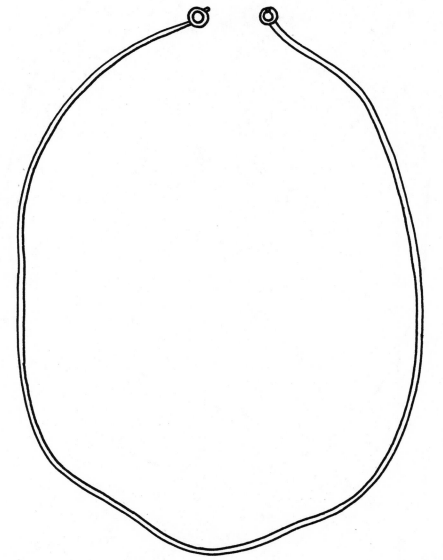

Name: _____

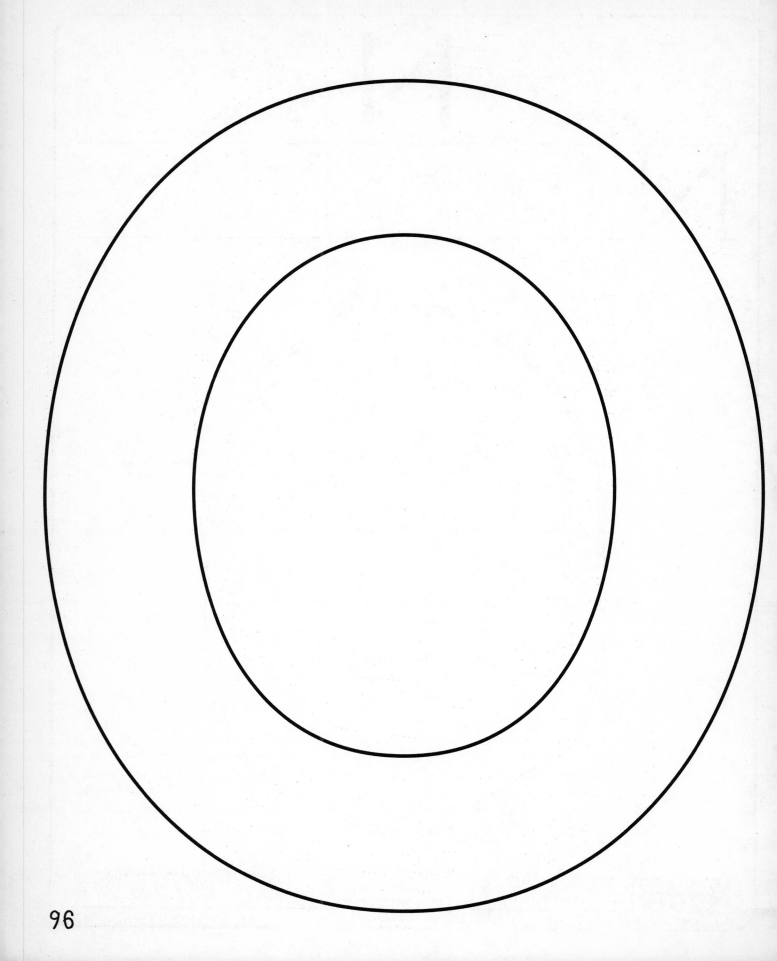

Name:_____

98

P

P P P P

Name:_____

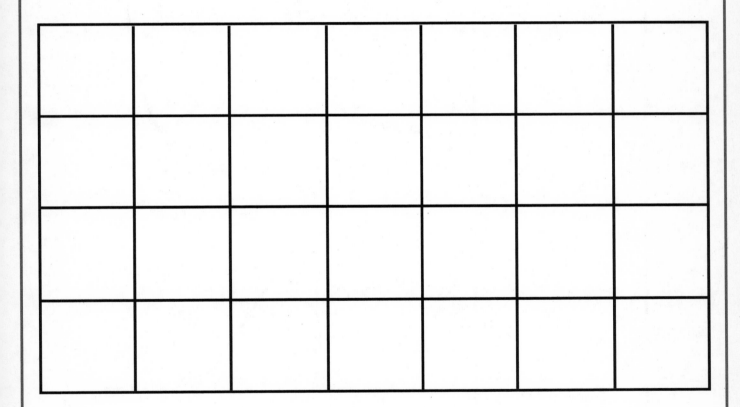

Name:_____

R

R R R R R

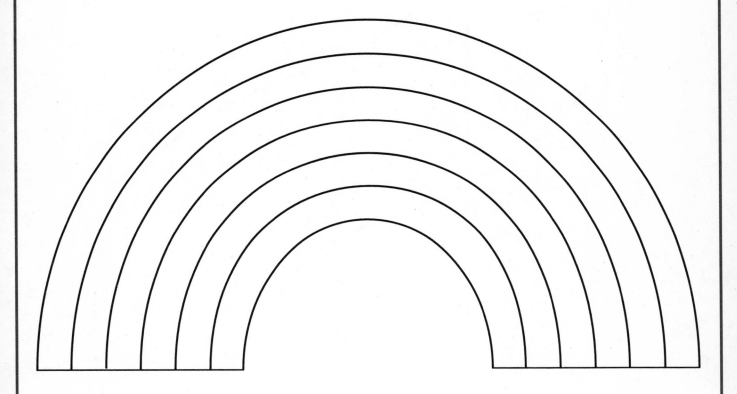

Name:_____

104

S

S S S S

Name:_____

106

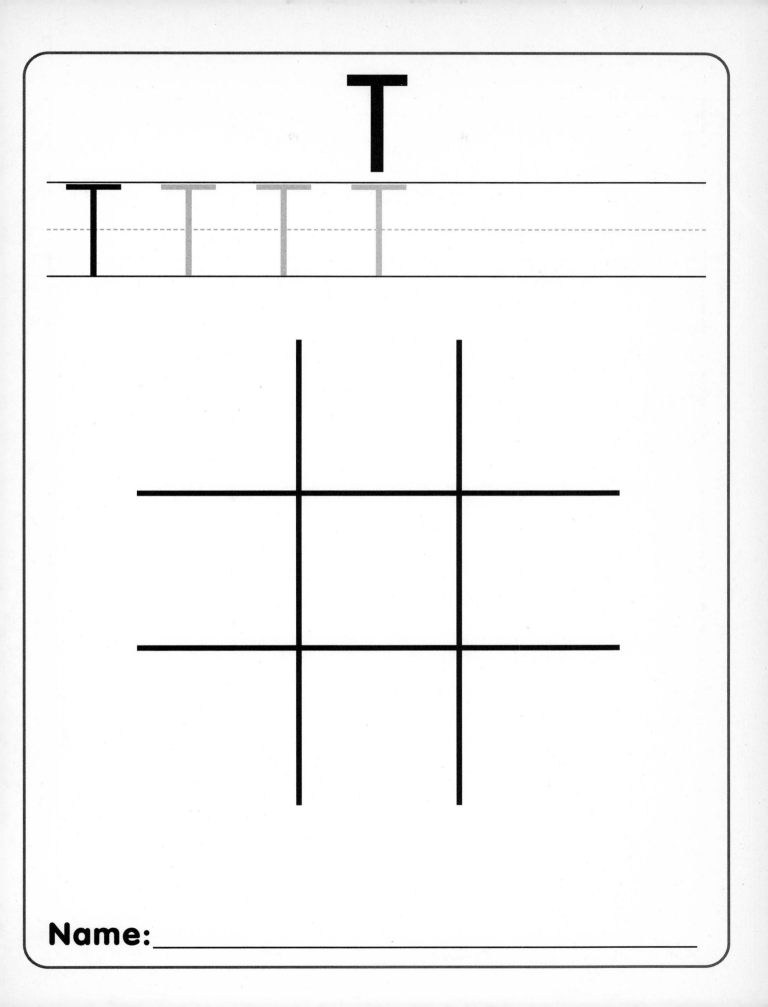

Name:_____

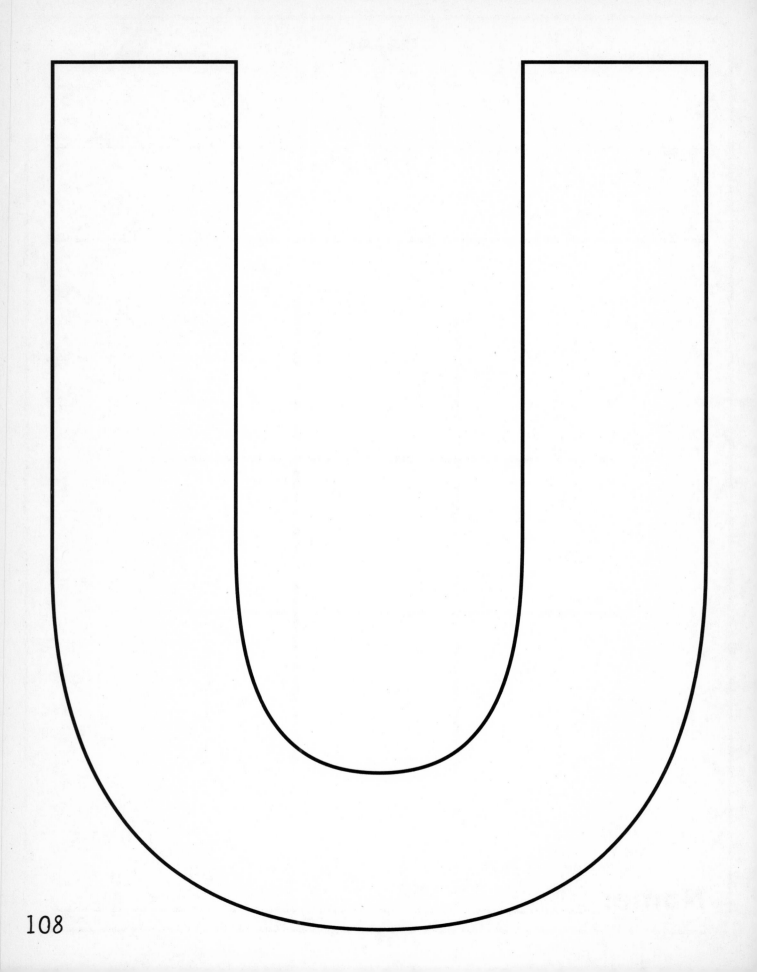

108

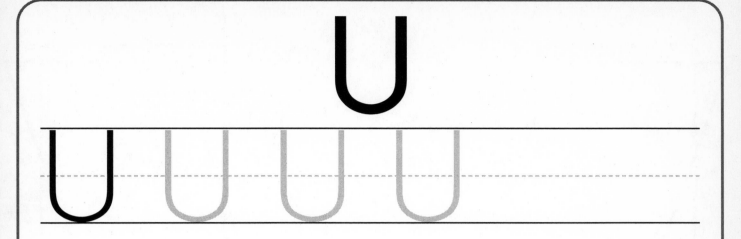

Name:_____

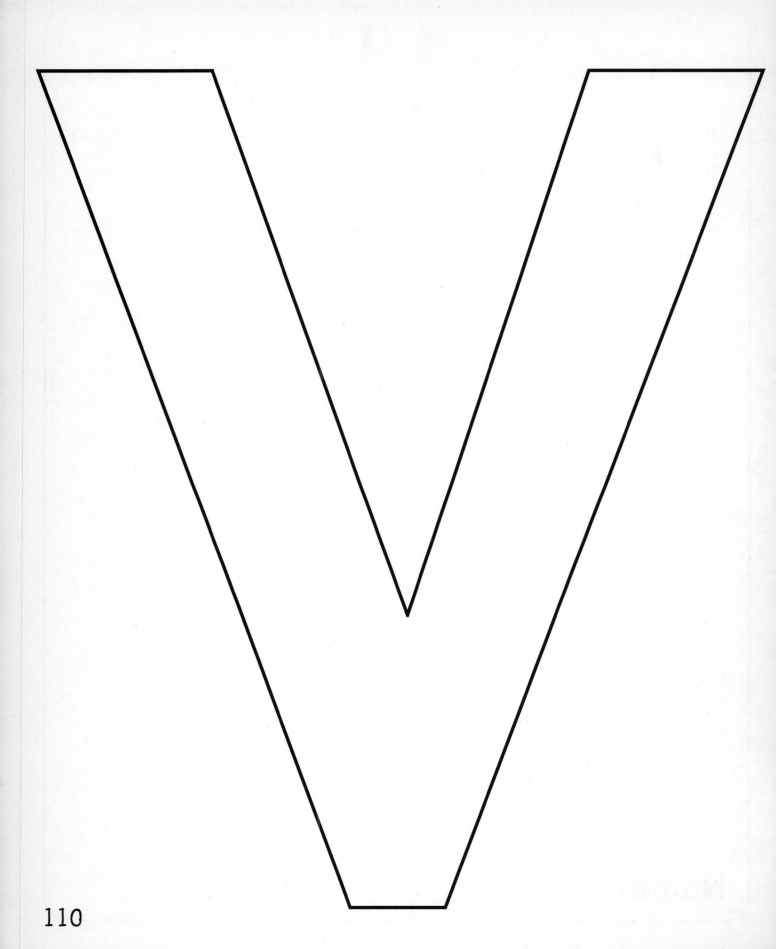

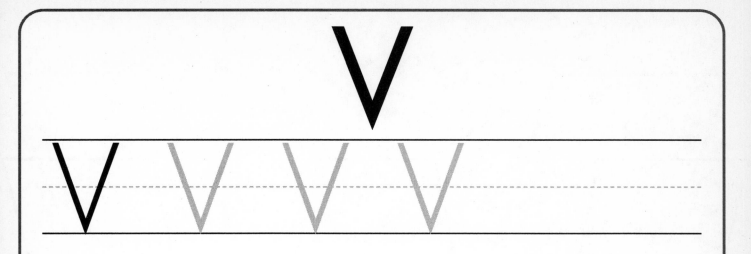

Name:_____

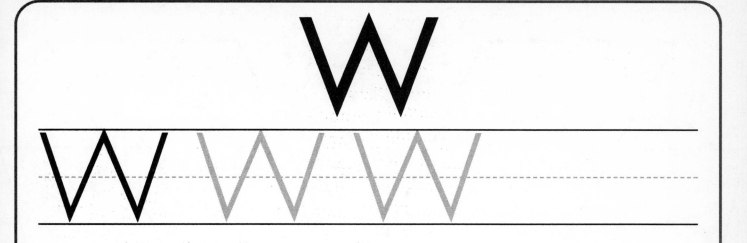

Name:_____

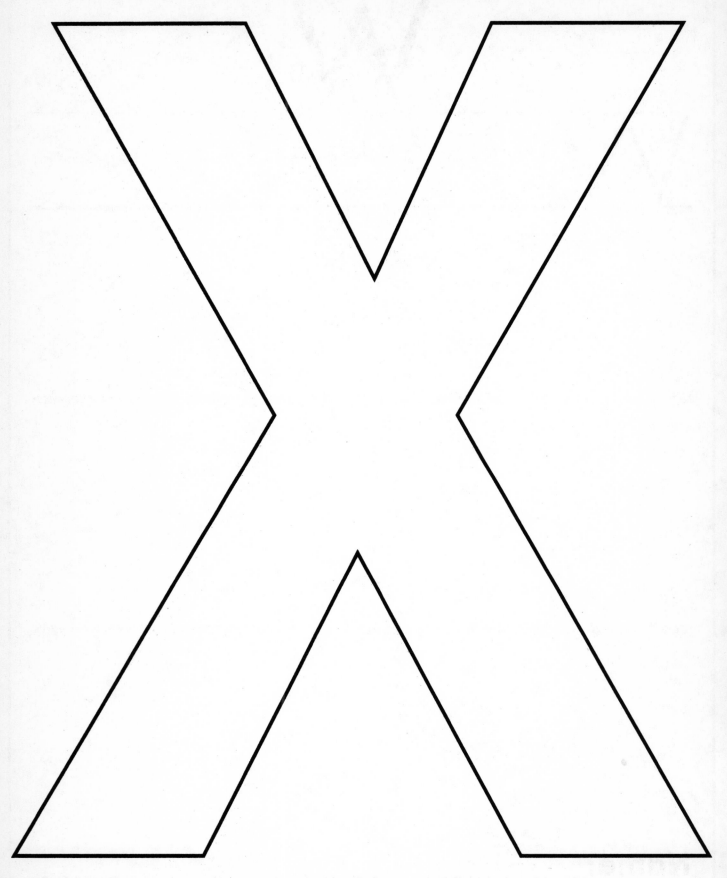

114

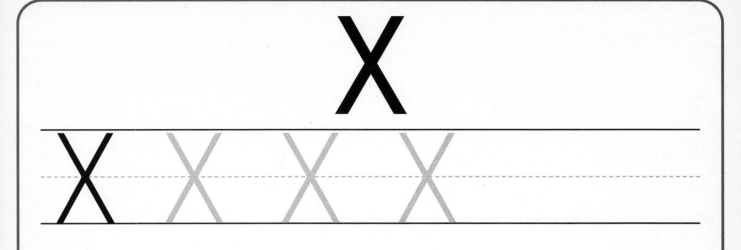

Name:_____

116

Y

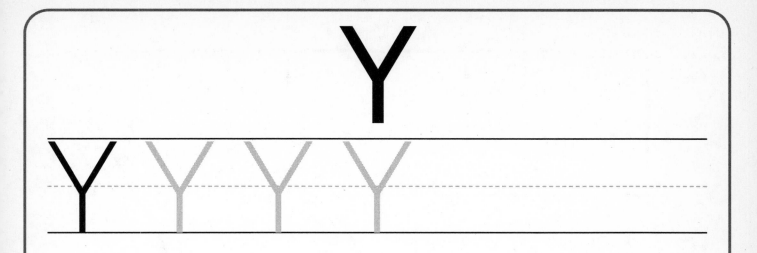

Name:_____

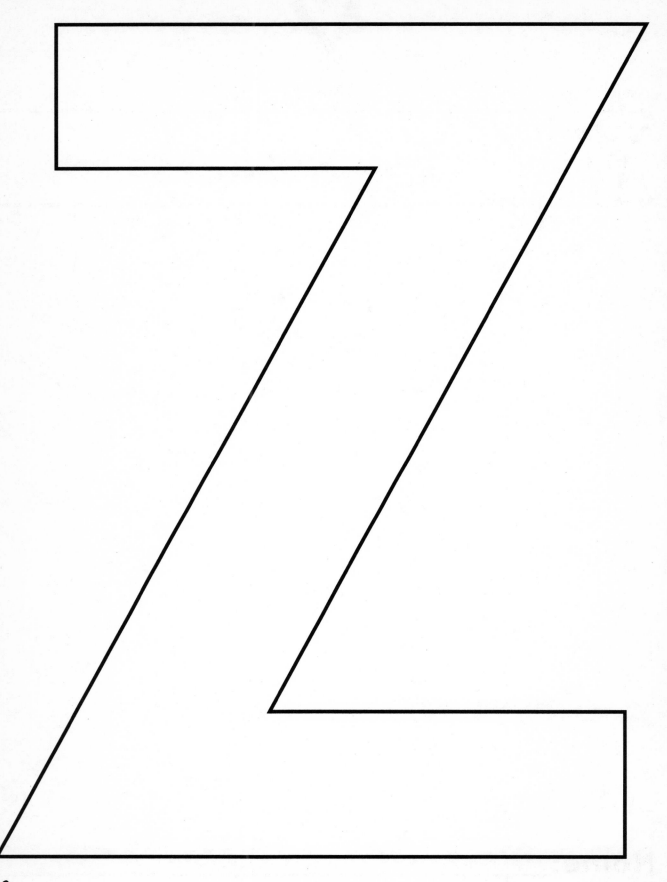

Z

Z Z Z Z Z

Name:_____

B

Balloon Pattern

D

Dinosaur Pattern

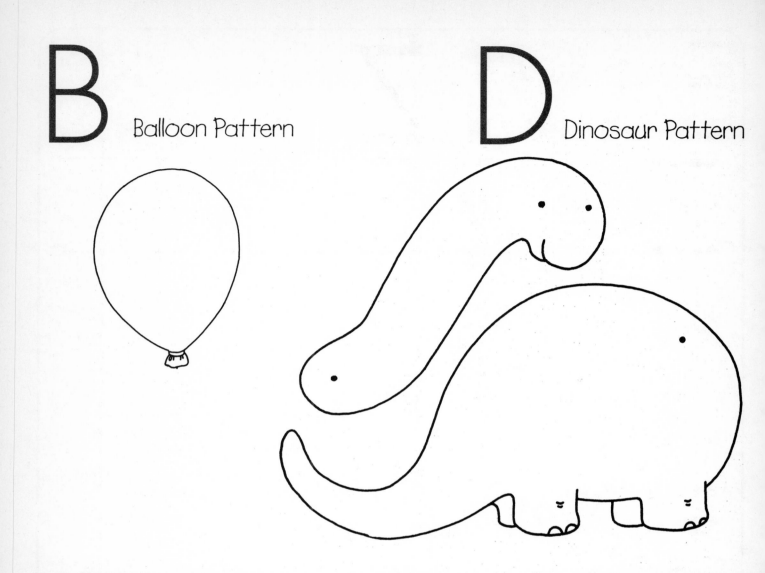

F

Fruit Pattern

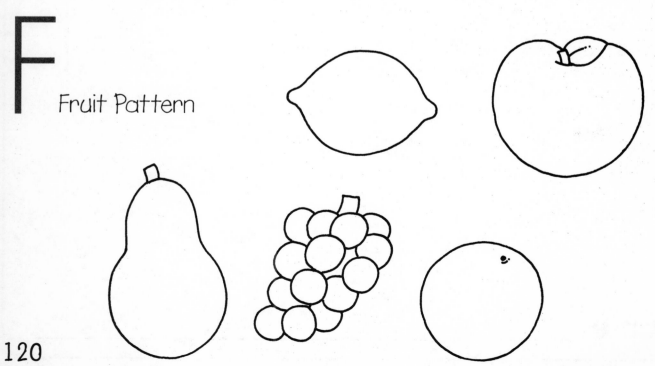

E

E Pictures

Elephant   Eagle   Easel

Egg   Ear   Eraser

F

Fruit Bowl Pattern

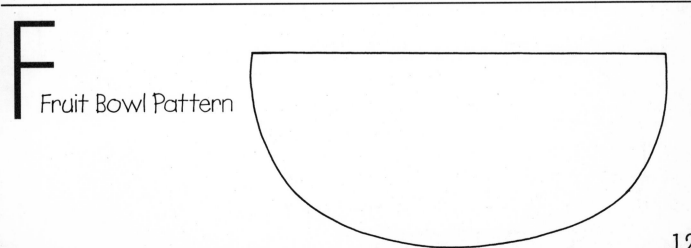

H House Pattern

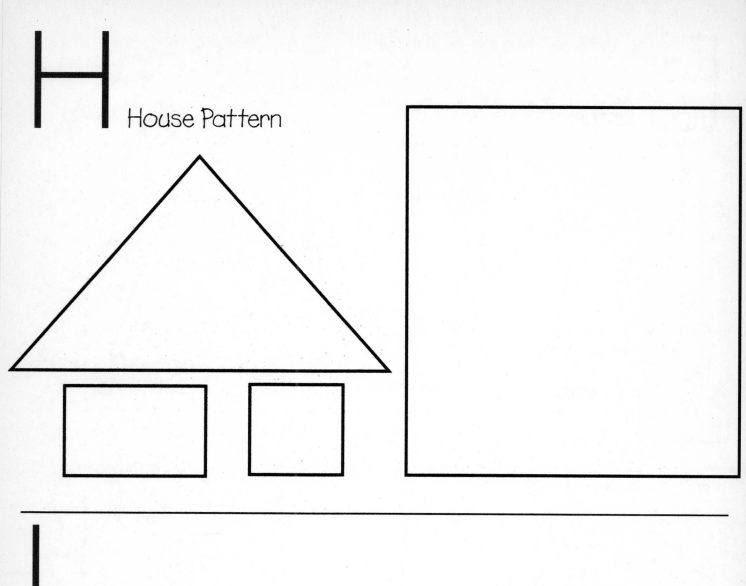

I Ice Cream Pattern

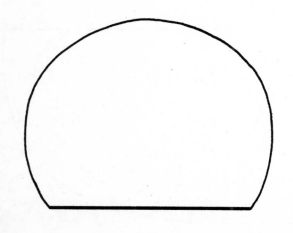

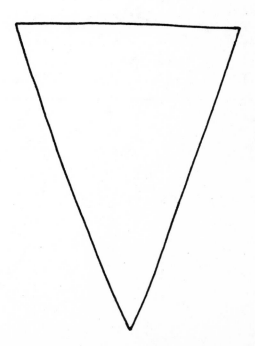

J

Jack -in-the Box Pattern

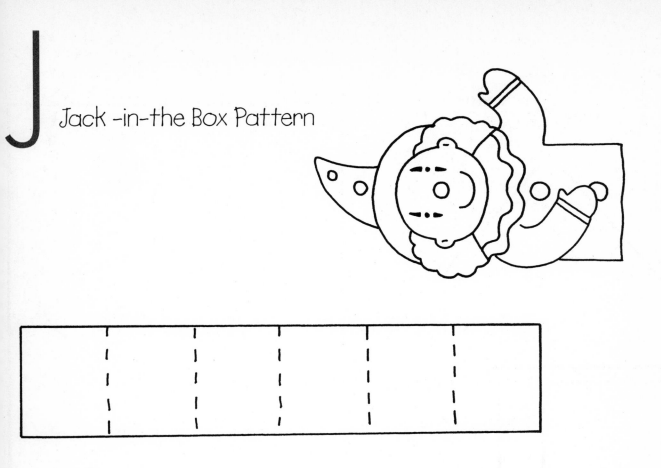

K

Kite Pattern

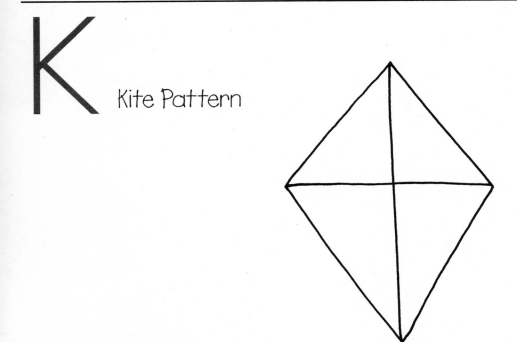

L Lion Pattern

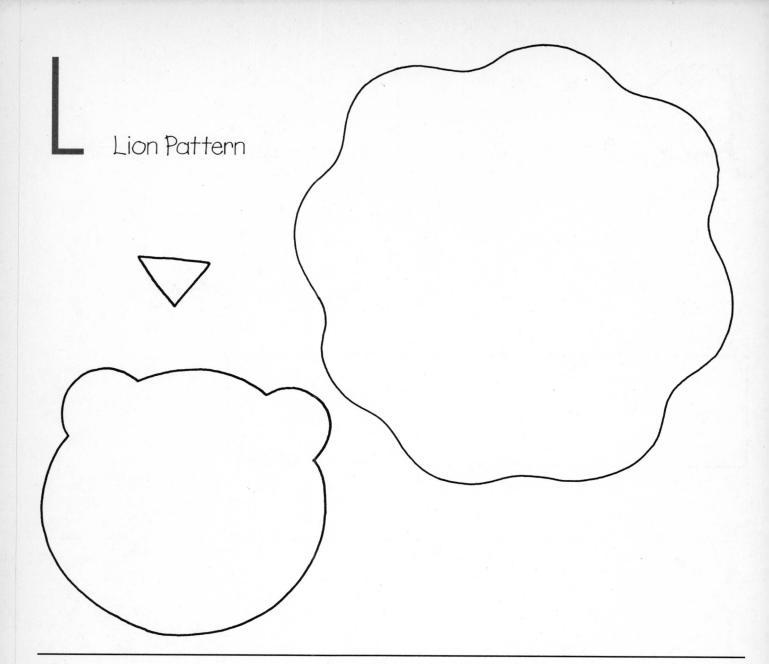

M Mitten Pattern

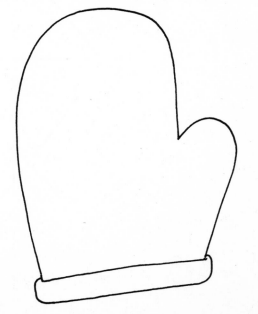

O Octopus Pattern

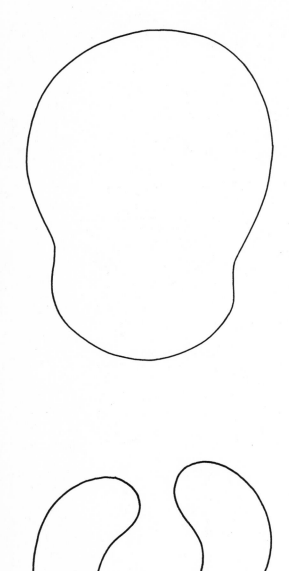

S Snowman Hat Pattern

W Whale Pattern

U Underwear Pattern

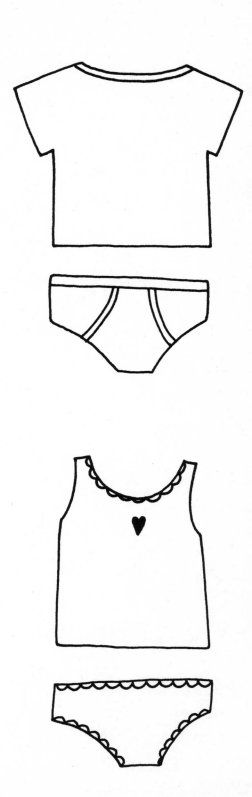

V

Van Pattern

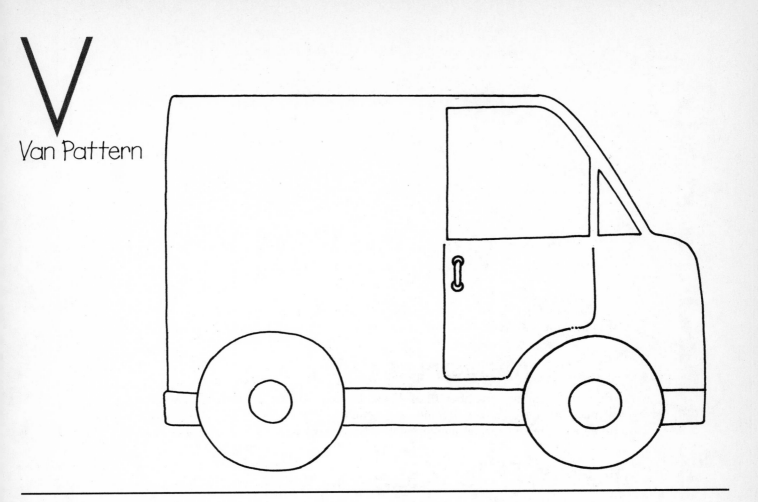

Z

Z Pictures

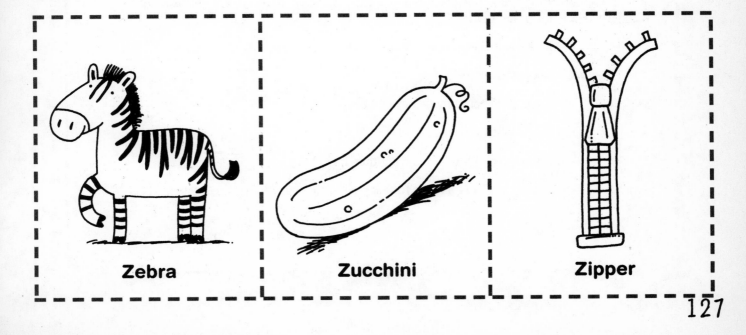

Zebra

Zucchini

Zipper

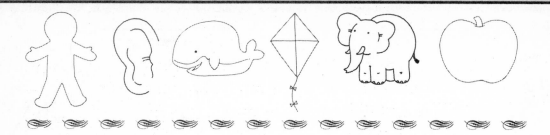

We Did It!

It's been a long trip through the alphabet, and the children acquired many new skills along the way. Here are some ways to wrap up the alphabet:

Share Memories

Take a moment to remember all of this hard work with the children. Talk about how much you have learned together since you began with the letter A. Invite children to share any special memories they have about making their alphabet books.

Add a Title Page

Before sending the children's alphabet books home, add a title page that lists everything included in your books. (See page 13.) You may want to add the name of the school and/or your classroom as well as the year the book was made.

Celebrate the Alphabet

It's a great time for a celebration. Have a "WE DID IT!" party or a Publishing Party. Here are some ideas:

- Make alphabet-shape invitations to send to parents and friends.
- Make alphabet soup.
- Bake alphabet pretzels or alphabet cookies.
- Sing alphabet songs.
- Have the children share what they have learned.
- Make I DID IT! badges for each child to wear.